Pallab Dasgupta
P. P. Chakrabarti
S. C. DeSarkar

**Multiobjective
Heuristic Search**

Computational Intelligence
edited by Wolfgang Bibel and Rudolf Kruse

The books in this series contribute to the long-range goal of understanding and realizing intelligent behaviour in some environment. Thus they cover topics from the disciplines of Artificial Intelligence and Cognitive Science, combined also called Intellectics, as well as from fields interdisciplinarily related with these. Computational Intelligence comprises basic knowledge as well as applications.

Das rechnende Gehirn
by Patricia S. Churchland and Terrence J. Sejnowski

Neuronale Netze und Fuzzy-Systeme
by Detlef Nauck, Frank Klawonn and Rudolf Kruse

Fuzzy-Clusteranalyse
by Frank Höppner, Frank Klawonn and Rudolf Kruse

Einführung in Evolutionäre Algorithmen
by Volker Nissen

Neuronale Netze
by Andreas Scherer

Sehen und die Verarbeitung visueller Informationen
by Hanspeter A. Mallot

Betriebswirtschaftliche Anwendungen des Soft Computing
by Biethahn et al. (Ed.)

Fuzzy Theorie und Stochastik
by Rudolf Seising (Ed.)

Multiobjective Heuristic Search
by Pallab Dasgupta, P. P. Chakrabarti and S. C. DeSarkar

Among others the following books were published
in the series of Artificial Intelligence

Automated Theorem Proving
by Wolfgang Bibel (out of print)

Fuzzy Sets and Fuzzy Logic
Foundation of Application – from a Mathematical Point of View
by Siegfried Gottwald

Fuzzy Systems in Computer Science
edited by Rudolf Kruse, Jörg Gebhard and Rainer Palm

Automatische Spracherkennung
by Ernst Günter Schukat-Talamazzini

Deduktive Datenbanken
by Armin B. Cremers, Ulrike Griefhahn and Ralf Hinze

Wissensrepräsentation und Inferenz
by Wolfgang Bibel, Steffen Hölldobler and Torsten Schaub

Vieweg

Pallab Dasgupta
P. P. Chakrabarti
S. C. DeSarkar

Multiobjective Heuristic Search

An Introduction to intelligent
Search Methods for
Multicriteria Optimization

1st Edition 1999

All rights reserved
© Friedr. Vieweg & Sohn Verlagsgesellschaft mbH, Braunschweig/Wiesbaden, 1999
translated by Brad Willard.

Vieweg is a subsidiary company of Bertelsmann Professional Information.

 No part of this publication may be reproduced, stored in a retrieval system or transmitted, mechanical, photocopying or otherwise without prior permission of the copyright holder.

Printing and binding: Lengericher Druckerei Hubert & Co., Göttingen
Printed on acid-free paper
Printed in Germany

ISBN 3-528-05708-4

Preface

A large number of problems require the optimization of multiple criteria. These criteria are often non-commensurate and sometimes conflicting in nature making the task of optimization more difficult. In such problems, the task of creating a combined optimization function is often not easy. Moreover, the decision procedure can be affected by the sensitivity of the solution space, and the trade-off is often non-linear. In real life we traditionally handle such problems by suggesting not one, but several non-dominated solutions. Finding a set of non-dominated solutions is also useful in multistaged optimization problems, where the solution of one stage of optimization is passed on to the next stage. One classic example is that of circuit design, where high-level synthesis, logic synthesis and layout synthesis comprise important stages of optimization of the circuit. Passing a set of non-dominated partial solutions from one stage to the next typically ensures better global optimization.

This book presents a new approach to multi-criteria optimization based on heuristic search techniques. Classical multicriteria optimization techniques rely on single criteria optimization algorithms, and hence we are either required to optimize one criterion at a time (under constraints on the others), or we are asked for a single scalar combined optimization function. On the other hand, the multiobjective search approach maps each optimization criterion onto a distinct dimension of a vector valued cost structure. A partial order relation is defined on the vector valued costs, and the search algorithm determines the set of solutions which are non-inferior with respect to the partial order. Thus each criterion retains its individual identity right through the optimization process.

The multiobjective search paradigm was proposed by Stewart and White in a paper (JACM,38,1991) where they introduced the notion of best-first search in a vector valued search space and presented the multiobjective generalization of the classical algorithm A^*. Subsequently, we have developed the foundations of multiobjective search on three different problem representation domains, namely, *state space search*, *problem reduction search*, and *game tree search*. This book is a compilation of our work on these topics.

The contents of this book are as follows. The first two chapters introduce the notion of multiobjective heuristic search and outline the work of Stewart and White. The third chapter presents our results on state space search and algorithms for memory bounded search in multiobjective state spaces. The fourth chapter outlines some of our applications of multiobjective heuristic search. The fifth and sixth chapters present our contributions on multiobjective problem reduction search and multiobjective game tree search respectively.

We acknowledge the financial support of Volkswagen Stiftung, Germany, for the publication of this book. We are deeply indebted to Professor Wolfgang Bibel for his support and encouragement. We thank Vieweg Verlag for publishing the book. We have used LaTeX for typesetting.

We are grateful to the Department of Computer Science and Engineering, Indian Institute of Technology Kharagpur, India, where we did the entire research on multiobjective heuristic search.

Pallab Dasgupta
P P Chakrabarti
S C DeSarkar

Contents

1 Introduction   1
    1.1 Multiobjective Search 2
       1.1.1 Contributions 3
    1.2 Organization of the book 7

2 The Multiobjective Search Model   9
    2.1 Popular Approaches 10
    2.2 The multiobjective approach 10
    2.3 The Multiobjective Search Problem 11
    2.4 Previous Work: *Multiobjective A** 13
    2.5 Conclusion 18

3 Multiobjective State Space Search   19
    3.1 Preliminary notations and definitions 20
    3.2 Multidimensional Pathmax 21
       3.2.1 The definition of *pathmax* 23
       3.2.2 Two basic properties of *pathmax* 23
       3.2.3 The significance of *pathmax* 24
    3.3 An induced total ordering: *K-ordering* 24
    3.4 The algorithm MOA** 27
       3.4.1 The Algorithm Outline 27

		3.4.2 Admissibility & Optimality	28
	3.5	Memory bounded multiobjective search	31
		3.5.1 Cost back-up and K-ordering	32
		3.5.2 General philosophy of MOMA*0	33
		3.5.3 Algorithm $MOMA^*0$	35
		3.5.4 Variants of MOMA*0	41
	3.6	Searching with inadmissible heuristics	43
	3.7	Extension to graphs	46
	3.8	Conclusion	47
4	**Applications of Multiobjective Search**		**49**
	4.1	The Operator Scheduling Problem	50
		4.1.1 Notation & Terminology	51
		4.1.2 Algorithm MObj_Schedule	53
	4.2	The Channel Routing Problem	57
		4.2.1 Notation & Terminology	60
		4.2.2 Algorithm MObj_Route	60
		4.2.3 Selection of wires for a track	63
	4.3	The Log Cutting problem	66
	4.4	Evaluation of the Multiobjective Strategies	67
		4.4.1 Utility of *Pathmax*	70
		4.4.2 Comparison of MOA** and ItrA*	70
		4.4.3 Comparison of MOMA*0 and DFBB	71
		4.4.4 Effect of multiple back-up costs in MOMA*0	72
5	**Multiobjective Problem Reduction Search**		**75**
	5.1	The problem definition	76
	5.2	The utility of K-ordering	79
	5.3	Selection using *pathmax* is NP-hard	81

	5.4	Selection for monotone heuristics	84
	5.5	The Algorithm: MObj*	86
	5.5.1	General philosophy of $MObj^*$	87
	5.5.2	Outline of MObj*	90
	5.5.3	Admissibility of MObj*	93
	5.5.4	Complexity of MObj*	95
	5.5.5	MObj* for OR-graphs	96
	5.6	Conclusion	96

6 Multiobjective Game Tree Search — 97

- 6.1 The problem definition — 99
- 6.2 Dominance Algebra — 107
- 6.3 Finding the packets — 109
- 6.4 Partial Order α-β Pruning — 113
  - 6.4.1 Shallow α-β pruning — 113
  - 6.4.2 Deep α-β pruning — 115
- 6.5 Conclusion — 118

7 Conclusion — 119

A — 125

- A.1 The outline of algorithm MOMA* — 125

Bibliography — 127

Chapter 1

Introduction

In the past three decades, researchers in the area of heuristic search have focussed on the central theme of *knowledge versus search* in some form or the other. The major attention has been towards quantifying problem specific knowledge in terms of a heuristic evaluation function and developing algorithmic frameworks for solving problems in an efficient manner. The nature of the heuristic function and its effect on the search mechanism has been a subject of considerable interest.

Heuristic search techniques have been developed for different problem representations, such as the *state space* representation, the *problem reduction* representation, and *game trees*. Classically heuristic search has been studied with two major objectives. The first has been to understand the relation between *heuristic accuracy* and *search complexity*. The other has been to develop *efficient* search algorithms for obtaining *optimal* and *suboptimal* solutions. In the process, heuristic search has been investigated under various situations. In particular, search has been studied for different types of heuristics such as admissible heuristics, inadmissible heuristics, non-monotone heuristics and weighted heuristics. The performance of heuristic search strategies have been analyzed for worst case and average case behaviors. Variants of the basic approach have been suggested to improve the performance of the search algorithms under different situations.

Most of the search schemes studied in the past assume that the criterion to be optimized is single and scalar valued. Consequently it is also assumed that there exists a total order on the costs evaluated at the various states of the problem. Best-first search algorithms such as A^* [69] use this total order to compare candidate search avenues and determine the potentially best path.

In this work we study a search framework called the multiobjective search framework, where the assumption regarding the existence of a total order among the costs is relaxed. Instead we consider the general situation where only a partial order exists among the costs. Since the model was originally proposed by Stewart and White [91] for extending heuristic search techniques to multicriteria optimization problems, the model has been named as the multiobjective search model. In the following sections, we briefly describe the multiobjective framework, and the major contributions of the work.

1.1 Multiobjective Search

Many real world optimization problems have multiple, conflicting non-commensurate objectives. The task of adequately modeling such problems in a search framework that is designed for optimizing single scalar functions is by no means easy, and has been the subject of considerable debate in the past [45]. One popular approach of solving such problems is to cast them into the conventional search framework after combining the multiple criteria into a single scalar criterion. However, in most multiobjective problems, the semantics of the desired solution is context dependent and can be dictated by individual preferences. Therefore, the task of constructing the combined evaluation function in a way so as to preserve the semantics of the desired solution is difficult, and may require sufficient experience about solving that problem.

The other popular approach of solving multiobjective problems is to optimize one criterion at a time under given constraints on the others. This approach automatically preserves the semantics of the problem since it allows the multiple dimensions to retain their individual identities. However, one difficulty lies in determining a set of good constraints, in the absence of which search becomes unduly expensive. Moreover, repeatedly searching the same state space by progressively refining the constraints (until a satisfactory solution is found) increases the search complexity enormously.

The multiobjective search model was introduced by Stewart and White [90, 91] as a unified framework for solving search problems involving multiple objectives. Since multiple non-commensurate criteria are involved, the solution space is partially ordered and will, in general, contain several *non-inferior* solutions. Multiobjective search addresses the task of determining the set of such solutions in the search space. Once the set of non-inferior solutions are found, standard procedures may be applied to choose the desired solution [5, 47, 52, 54, 67, 94].

In the multiobjective framework, the costs are modeled by vectors, such that each dimension of the cost represents a distinct non-commensurate optimization criterion. The following partial order is used to identify the non-inferior options.

Def # 1.1 Dominance :
Let $\vec{y}_1$ and $\vec{y}_2$ be two K-dimensional vectors. Then $\vec{y}_1$ dominates $\vec{y}_2$ iff:

1. *$\vec{y}_1$ is as good as $\vec{y}_2$ in all the K dimensions, and*
2. *$\vec{y}_1$ is better than $\vec{y}_2$ in at least one of the K dimensions.*

where good and better are defined in terms of the scalar valued criteria associated with

1.1 Multiobjective Search

the individual objectives. A vector $\vec{y}_i$ is said to be "non-dominated" in a set of vectors Y if there does not exist another vector $\vec{y}_j \in Y$ such that $\vec{y}_j$ dominates $\vec{y}_i$. □

A multiobjective search strategy uses the above partial order to eliminate all clearly inferior alternatives and direct the search towards the set of non-dominated solutions. The multiobjective heuristic search problem is as follows:

Def # 1.2 Multiobjective Search Problem :

Given:
1. *A search space, represented as a locally finite directed graph.*
2. *A vector valued cost structure, with each dimension representing a distinct optimization criterion.*
3. *A heuristic evaluation function that returns a set of non-dominated vector valued costs for each candidate search avenue. Each cost is an estimate of the cost of potential non-dominated solutions which may be obtained along that search avenue.*

Find:
The set of non-dominated solutions in the search space.

□

In their work [90, 91], Stewart and White presented an algorithm MOA^* which is a generalization of the well known A^* algorithm [69] to the multiobjective search framework.

1.1.1 Contributions

We summarize our major contributions in the following sub-sections.

Multiobjective State Space Search

In this work, several interesting results have been obtained in the area of multiobjective search of ordinary graphs [23, 21]. We briefly highlight the major contributions.

A. Searching under inadmissible heuristics: We have shown that if heuristics are allowed to overestimate, then no algorithm is guaranteed to find all non-dominated solutions unless it expands nodes having dominated costs also. This effectively implies that only brute force search techniques are admissible.

B. **Utility of Pathmax:** The use of the *pathmax* property to modify non-monotone heuristics and improve the performance of best-first search strategies such as A* is well known [25, 66, 10]. In this work, we show that the idea of *pathmax* can be extended to the multiobjective search domain also.

In the single objective search model, it has been shown [25] that the utility of *pathmax* in tree search is confined to *pathological* problem instances only, that is, in problem instances where *every* solution path contains at least one fully informed non-goal node. We show that in the multiobjective domain *pathmax* has a greater utility, since it can reduce the set of nodes expanded in non-pathological problem instances as well.

C. **Using an induced total order:** A characteristic feature of the multiobjective search problem is the existence of multiple non-dominated search avenues. In this work, we have investigated the utility of using an induced total order called *K-order* for selecting the search path and have obtained the following results:

1. If an induced total order is used to guide the search, then in general it is not necessary to evaluate all the heuristics vectors at a node. This result is useful for problems where generating the heuristics are costly.

2. When a best-first memory bounded strategy backtracks, it must back up the best cost from the pruned space. In the multiobjective search framework, the pruned space may contain a large number of non-dominated costs. We show that if an induced total order is used to guide the search then it is possible to back up only one of these costs and yet guarantee admissibility.

D. **New Multiobjective Search Strategies:** Two multiobjective search strategies have been developed.

Algorithm MOA:** By using the concept of *pathmax*, an extension of the algorithm MOA* has been developed which is superior in terms of node expansions. This algorithm called MOA** also uses an induced total ordering for selection.

Algorithm MOMA*0: This is a generalized memory bounded strategy that expands the same set of nodes as MOA** and operates in linear space. Several variants of this algorithm have been studied.

Applications

We have modeled three problems using the multiobjective framework and studied the performance of the search algorithms developed in this work. The first two are well known problems in the area of VLSI design [18]. The third is a variant of the bin packing problem. The problems addressed are:

The Operator Scheduling Problem: This problem appears in VLSI high level synthesis [65], where *area* and *delay* of a design are two non-commensurate objectives.

1.1 Multiobjective Search

The Channel Routing Problem: This is a problem of VLSI layout synthesis [26], where *the number of tracks* (representing area) and *the number of vias* (representing delay through a net) are two non-commensurate objectives.

The Log Cutting Problem: This is a variant of the bin packing problem with two objectives [29]. One objective is to optimize the number of logs being cut to deliver a set of slices of various sizes. The other is to optimize the number of cutting patterns (which reflects the number of times the blade positions have to be altered).

The algorithms developed in this work have been applied to the above problems. The observations obtained from these applications empirically establish the following:

1. If the heuristics are non-monotonic, then the number of nodes expanded is reduced if *pathmax* is used to strengthen the heuristics.

2. Algorithm MOA** is superior to other policies such as ItrA* (that is, iteratively applying A^*) and DFBB (that is, depth-first branch and bound) in terms of number of node expansions. In the presence of space constraints, the linear space strategy MOMA*0 is superior to DFBB.

Multiobjective Problem Reduction Search

Popular best-first problem reduction search strategies such as AO^* adopt the policy of expanding only those nodes that belong to *potential solution graphs* (*psg*) whose cost is less than the cost of the optimal solution graph. A natural approach would be to extend this policy to the multiobjective search framework, where only nodes belonging to non-dominated cost *psg*s are expanded. However, in this work we have been able to establish the following result [19, 22] that presents an entirely different scenario from that of the single objective problem:

- *Given an explicit additive AND/OR graph, the task of identifying a non-dominated cost psg is NP-hard in general. Several variants have also been shown to be NP-hard.*

Since the complexity of the task of identifying the minimum cost *psg* in an explicit single objective additive AND/OR graph is polynomial in the number of nodes in the graph, the complexity of AO^* is polynomial in the number of nodes it expands. In the multiobjective framework, the above result shows that unless $P = NP$, there cannot be any strategy whose complexity is polynomial in Q, where Q denotes the set of the nodes belonging to non-dominated cost *psg*s. In this background the following algorithm has been developed for searching AND/OR graphs.

Algorithm M_Obj*: The proposed algorithm is a best-first strategy that operates in linear space and has a time complexity of O(T^2), where T is defined as follows:

$$T = \sum_{n \in Q} CARD(P(n))$$

CARD(P(n)) denotes the number of maximal non-dominated *psg*s P(n) with n as a tip node.

Search of Multiobjective Game Trees

Current game tree searching methods assume that the merit of a given position of the game can be evaluated as a single numerical value. In normal two-player games, a MIN-MAX value [75] is defined, that indicates the best alternative available to a player. Depth-first algorithms like α-β *pruning* [46] and best-first algorithms like *SSS** [92] are known to efficiently determine this MIN-MAX value. These studies have also been extended to multiplayer games [49].

In the present work, we have studied an interesting variant of the game tree searching problem where the information available amongst the players is a partial order. The cost evaluated at every position of the game is modeled as a vector. Each dimension of the cost vector represents a distinct criterion of merit. The decision making *strategy* of a player is defined as a mapping from the set of vector valued outcomes to a totally ordered set, which is consistent with the partial order. Our contributions [20, 24] are as follows:

A. Non-inferior sets of outcomes: If the opponent's strategy is not known, then corresponding to every strategy of the player, there will be a set of possible outcomes depending on the strategy adopted by the opponent. We have identified the necessary and sufficient conditions for a *set* of outcomes to be inferior to another set of outcomes. We also show that unless the strategies of both players are known, it may be necessary to back up all sets of non-inferior outcomes.

B. Dominance Algebra: We have constructed an algebra called *Dominance Algebra* to describe the relation between the sets of outcomes backed up at a node. We have shown that the set of non-inferior options of a player can be represented as a minimal expression of the proposed algebra.

C. Pruning Conditions: We have identified both deep and shallow pruning conditions for multiobjective game trees. These conditions lead to the construction of α-*expressions* and β-*expressions* using dominance algebra, which are somewhat similar to the α and β bounds in α-β pruning.

D. Partial Order α-β: Using the proposed pruning conditions, a partial order search strategy has been developed on lines similar to the α-β strategy for conventional game trees.

1.2 Organization of the book

The book is organized as follows.

Chapter 2: Chapter 2 describes the multiobjective search model in detail and presents previous work on multiobjective heuristic search that forms the background of our work. The chapter describes the multiobjective generalization of A* proposed by Stewart *et al* [91].

Chapter 3: Our contributions in multiobjective state space search is presented in this chapter. The utility of using *pathmax* in the multiobjective domain is shown. The idea of using an induced total order (called *K-order*) is introduced. Based on these, the algorithm MOA** is presented. Issues related to inadmissible heuristics are considered. The problem of multiobjective state space search under memory constraints is addressed. A recursive linear space best-first multiobjective search strategy MOMA*0 is presented. Several variants of the proposed algorithm are suggested.

Chapter 4: This chapter contains the modeling and implementation of three practical problems using the multiobjective model.

Chapter 5: Multiobjective problem reduction search has been studied in this chapter. We prove that the problem of identifying a non-dominated cost *psg* is NP-hard in general. Strategies for solving the problem under such situations lead to the development of the search algorithm $MObj^*$.

Chapter 6: This chapter concerns multiobjective game tree search. The chapter analyzes the semantics of the partial order game tree search problem. The idea of using *Dominance Algebra* to represent the options of a player is introduced, following which the partial order pruning conditions are identified. The chapter concludes by presenting a partial order α-β pruning strategy.

Chapter 7: The conclusion of the book is presented in this chapter.

Chapter 2

The Multiobjective Search Model

In the course of applying heuristic search techniques to practical problems, several issues have assumed significance. Some of these issues have evolved from practical considerations such as space and time constraints, that are directly related to the feasibility of the existing search techniques. Other issues have gained importance through the requirements of frameworks for modeling problems from specific domains in a more realistic manner and solving them efficiently. The multiobjective search model is one such framework for modeling and solving search problems involving multiple, conflicting and non-commensurate optimization criteria.

The subject of multicriteria decision making has been well studied in operations research [3, 12, 15, 33, 34, 35, 42, 70, 88, 89, 98, 100]. In multicriteria decision making, it is assumed that a small set of alternatives are available from which a selection must be made on the basis of multiple factors of merit. Often *Multi-Attribute Utility Theory (MAUT)* is used to create a scalar-valued criterion for selecting from the decision set [2, 12, 13, 27, 33, 45, 56, 86, 96, 99]. Since the individual preferences of the decision maker is of prime importance in multicriteria decision making, many researchers have approached the problem using interactive methods [5, 7, 30, 32, 47, 52, 53, 55, 58, 67, 78, 94, 95, 98, 97].

Multicriteria optimization problems have often been approached by generalizing standard operations research methods. Multiobjective versions of the simplex method have been developed for solving multiobjective linear programming problems [33, 76, 99]. Multiobjective dynamic programming has also been investigated [8, 17, 36, 37].

A multiobjective heuristic search model was proposed by Stewart and White [90, 91] with the intention of extending heuristic search techniques to multicriteria optimization problems. In this section we present a brief outline of the search model and the work of

Stewart and White. Before describing the search model, we give a short sketch of popular search based approaches to multiobjective optimization problems as a background to the multiobjective search scheme.

2.1 Popular Approaches

Almost the entire gamut of work done in the domain of heuristic search assume that the criterion to be optimized is single and scalar valued. Most search strategies attempt to find a solution that is good with respect to the single criterion under consideration. The task of adequately modeling multicriteria problems in a framework that has been designed for optimizing a single criterion is often not easy, and has been the subject of considerable debate in the past [45]. The popular approaches used [28] are to combine the criteria to form a single criterion, or to optimize one criterion at a time under given constraints on the others. We briefly discuss the drawbacks of each approach from the point of view of heuristic search.

Combining the criteria: If multiple criteria are present then it is unlikely in general that the search space will contain an undisputed *best* solution that is better than all other solutions in every criterion of merit. Moreover, if the criteria are non-commensurate (such as area, delay, power and testability in VLSI circuit design problems), then the desired solution may depend on individual preferences based on the context in which the problem is being solved. The difficulty often lies in developing a combined evaluation function that conveys the semantics of the desired solution to the search mechanism before knowing the set of possible alternative solutions.

Optimizing one criterion at a time under constraints on the others: This is a natural approach for solving multidimensional problems, since it preserves the identity of each dimension of the problem. However as the set of solutions in the search space is not known a priori, it is difficult to determine strong constraints that demarcate the most desired solution from the others. If the constraints are weak, then the solution found may not be the most desired solution based on the individual preferences of the problem solver. In such cases, the popular approach is to progressively refine the constraints until a suitable solution is found. Therefore, this approach requires several explorations into the search space and may turn out to be computationally very expensive.

2.2 The multiobjective approach

The multiobjective search model is motivated from the fact that often it is much more easier to choose the desired solution (based on individual preferences) from a given set of non-inferior solutions, than to describe the semantics of the desired solution without knowing the set of possible solutions. The set of non-inferior solutions can be found without any knowledge about the individual preferences of the problem solver. Given, the set of non-dominated alternatives, standard techniques are known for deciding the *most preferred* alternative based on individual preferences [5, 47, 52, 54, 67, 94].

The aim of multiobjective search is to determine the set of non-inferior solutions in the search space, so that known methods can be applied thereafter to select the desired solution. The approach of determining the set of non-dominated alternatives also has other distinct advantages some of which are as follows:

Search space exploration: Instead of repeated explorations of the search space under progressively refined constraints, it may be more efficient to determine the set of non-inferior solutions in a single exploration, and then select the most desirable solution.

Solving the same problem under different contexts: In the case of problems that need to be solved from time to time under different contexts for different non-inferior solutions, it may be useful to determine the entire set of non-inferior solutions in one pass.

Multistaged problem solving: Real world problems are often so complex that they have to be broken down into smaller and feasible problems. This has led to multistaged problem solving approaches. In multistaged approaches, the solutions of a stage define the constraints on the latter stages. Thus corresponding to every solution of a given stage different solutions will exist at the latter stages. In order to guarantee that the complete solution is non-inferior, all such alternatives need to be considered, and therefore it is pertinent to pass the entire set of non-inferior solutions of a stage to the next stage.

2.3 The Multiobjective Search Problem

The multiobjective search model is an extension of the conventional search model that accommodates a multi-dimensional cost structure. Each dimension of the vector valued cost structure models a distinct criterion to be optimized. The objective is to identify the set of non-dominated solutions in the search space. A given solution is said to be non-dominated if there is no other solution in the search space which is as good as the given solution in every dimension and better in at least one of the dimensions. The primary differences of this framework from the standard search model are as follows:

A. Vector valued costs: The cost structure is vector valued where each dimension of the cost vector represents a distinct criterion to be optimized.

B. Multiple non-inferior solutions: The objective of the multiobjective search paradigm is to determine the entire set of non-inferior solutions in the search space.

C. Heuristic function returning a set of costs: In the multiobjective search space, a given node may lie on the path to more than one non-dominated solution. For every solution path that contains the given node, the multiobjective heuristic function computes a vector valued estimate of the corresponding solution cost. It should be noted that some of these vectors computed at the node may not be distinct since the same vector may estimate the cost vectors of more than one solution. However if a single vector were to estimate the cost vectors of all the solutions then the heuristic value would become overtly restrictive. Therefore, a typical multiobjective heuristic function computes a set of non-dominated heuristic vectors at every node.

The selection mechanism in multiobjective search is based on the *dominance relation* which defines a partial order on the cost vectors. The relation is based on the simple assumption that clearly inferior alternatives (that is, those which are inferior to other alternatives in all the criteria) can be eliminated. The formal definition of *dominance* in the multiobjective state space representation is as follows:

Def # 2.1 (The Dominance Relation:) *Let y^1 and y^2 be two K-dimensional vectors. We define two types of dominance, namely* loose dominance *and* strict dominance. y^1 *"loosely dominates" y^2 iff:*

$$y_i^1 \leq y_i^2 \qquad \forall i, \ 1 \leq i \leq K$$

and y^1 "strictly dominates" y^2 iff:

$$y_i^1 \leq y_i^2 \qquad \forall i, \ 1 \leq i \leq K \text{ and } y^1 \neq y^2$$

Throughout this study, whenever we consider the dominance of the cost vector of a solution over any other cost vector, we refer to "loose dominance". For all other cost comparisons, we refer to "strict dominance". A vector $y \in Y$ is said to be "non-dominated" (in Y / by Y) if there does not exist another vector $y' \in Y$ such that y' dominates y. □

The reason for defining two types of dominance is as follows. When nodes in the state space are being compared on the basis of their cost vectors it is not justifiable to use "loose dominance" to determine the non-dominated set, since nodes having similar cost vectors are equally eligible for further consideration. In such cases "strict dominance" should be used to evaluate the non-dominated set of cost vectors. On the other hand, if a given cost vector of a node equals the cost vector of a solution which has been found already, and if the heuristics are admissible (that is, underestimates in each dimension), then there is no justification in further considering that cost vector. Therefore, when comparing the cost vector of a node with the cost vector of a solution, "loose dominance" is appropriate. It should also be noted that when we address the problem of finding the set of non-dominated solutions, the objective is to determine non-dominated solutions with distinct cost vectors only and therefore we require the concept of "loose dominance".

The multiobjective heuristic search problem is as follows:

The Multiobjective Search Problem:

Given:
1. A problem state space, represented as a locally finite directed graph.
2. A single start node in the graph.
3. A finite set of goal nodes in the graph.
4. A positive vector-valued cost associated with each arc in the graph.
5. A heuristic evaluation function that returns a set of vectors at each node.

To Find:
The set of non-dominated solution paths in the graph.

2.4 Previous Work: *Multiobjective A**

The algorithm MOA* of Stewart and White [91] is an elegant extension of the algorithm A* which works on the same basic principle with suitable modifications to address the multiobjective search problem. We describe this algorithm with an example so as to highlight the basic issues involved in multiobjective best-first search.

The characteristic features of the algorithm MOA^* are as follows:

- As in the case of A*, the algorithm MOA* uses a set OPEN for storing the nodes that are candidates for expansion and a set CLOSED to store the nodes which have been expanded already.

- At each node n the heuristic evaluation function computes a set $H(n)$ of heuristic vectors.

- Since in the multiobjective state space there may exist more than one non-dominated cost path from s to a node n, it becomes necessary to allow for multiple non-dominated cost vectors between s and n. Therefore MOA* uses a set $G(n)$ to represent the set of path cost vectors from s to n, and LABEL sets for accommodating possible multiple backpointers from the node n.

- Like A*, MOA* uses the sum of the accrued cost and the heuristic estimate to evaluate the potential of a node. For this purpose it constructs a set $F(n)$ of cost vectors at a node n by successively adding up each vector in $G(n)$ with the heuristic vectors in $H(n)$ and eliminating the dominated cost vectors.

- To capture the multiple non-dominated solutions during the course of search, the algorithm MOA* uses three lists, namely SOLUTION, SOLUTION_GOALS and SOLUTION_COSTS. Whenever a non-dominated cost goal node is encountered, it is inserted in SOLUTION_GOALS and its cost vector is inserted in SOLUTION_COSTS. Before terminating, MOA* identifies each non-dominated solution path by backtracing from the nodes in SOLUTION_GOALS along the backpointers. These solution paths are saved in the list SOLUTION.

The basic iteration of the algorithm consists of the selection of a non-dominated node from OPEN, generation of its successors and entering them in OPEN or CLOSED. A node n in OPEN is considered to be a candidate for expansion if its heuristic set $H(n)$ contains a cost vector which is non-dominated by the cost vectors of all solutions and by every cost vector of the other nodes in OPEN. MOA* maintains a list called ND which stores the set of non-dominated nodes in OPEN. We outline the algorithm MOA* below:

Algorithm MOA*

1. **[INITIALIZE]**
    OPEN ← s ; SOLUTION_GOALS ← ϕ ;
    CLOSED ← ϕ ; SOLUTION_COSTS ← ϕ ;
    SOLUTION ← ϕ ; LABEL ← ϕ ;

2. **[FIND ND]**
    Find the set of nodes in OPEN, call it ND, that have at least one cost vector that is not dominated by:
    2.1 The cost vector of any solution path already discovered (in SOLUTION_COSTS) nor by,
    2.2 The cost vector of any other potential solution represented by a node in OPEN.

3. **[TERMINATE]**
    If ND is empty, do the following:
    3.1 Use the set of preferred solution path cost vectors in SOLUTION_COSTS and the LABEL sets, if any, to trace through backpointers from the goal nodes in SOLUTION_GOALS to s.
    3.2 Place solution paths in SOLUTION.
    3.3 Terminate.

4. **[SELECT]**
    If ND is nonempty, do the following:
    4.1 Use a domain specific heuristic to choose a node n from ND for expansion, taking goals, if any, first.
    4.2 Remove n from OPEN.
    4.3 Place n on CLOSED.
    4.4 Do bookkeeping to maintain accrued costs and node selection function values.

5. **[IDENTIFY SOLUTIONS]**
    If n is a goal node, do the following:
    5.1 Add it to SOLUTION_GOALS.
    5.2 Add its current cost vectors to SOLUTION_COSTS.
    5.3 Remove any dominated members of SOLUTION_COSTS.
    5.4 Goto [Step 2].

2.4 Previous Work: Multiobjective A*

6. **[EXPAND]**
    Expand n and examine its successors.
    6.1 Generate the successors of n.
    6.2 If n has no successors, Goto [Step 2].
    6.3 Otherwise, for each successor n' of n, do the following:
        6.3.1 If $n' \notin OPEN$ and $n' \notin CLOSED$ then:
            6.3.1.1 Establish a backpointer from n' to n. Set $LABEL(n, n')$
                equal to the non-dominated subset of the set of accrued costs
                of paths through n to n' that have been discovered so far.
            6.3.1.2 Establish a non-dominated accrued cost set, $G(n') = LABEL(n', n)$.
            6.3.1.3 Compute node selection values, $F(n')$, using $G(n')$ and $H(n')$.
            6.3.1.4 Add n' to OPEN.
        6.3.2 Otherwise, n' was previously generated. If any potentially
            non-dominated paths to n' have been discovered, then, for each one,
            do the following:
            6.3.2.1 Ensure that its cost vector is in $LABEL(n', n)$ and
                therefore in the current set of non-dominated accrued
                costs of paths discovered so far to n', that is, in $G(n')$.
            6.3.2.2 If a new cost vector was added to $G(n')$ then:
                6.3.2.2.1 Purge from $LABEL(n', n)$ those vectors associated
                    with paths to n' to which the new path is
                    strictly preferred.
                6.3.2.2.2 If n' was on CLOSED, move it to OPEN.

7. **[ITERATE]**
    Goto [Step 2].

It may be observed that if MOA* is applied to a single objective problem, then its operation is the same as that of A*. In their paper, Stewart and White [91] used *"strict dominance"* only. In that case MOA*, when applied to single objective problems, would behave like a variant of A* which finds all optimal cost paths. However, if in step 5.4 of MOA* the statement "Goto [Step 2]" is replaced by "Terminate", then it would again behave exactly like A*. To illustrate the operation of algorithm MOA* on a multiobjective graph, we consider the following example.

Example # 2.1 Consider the graph of Fig 2.1. The graph represents a simple two-objective state space graph. The 2-dimensional vector valued costs of the edges of the state space graph are shown besides the edges. The heuristic vectors at a node are simply defined as the non-dominated set of cost vectors corresponding to the outgoing edges from that node. The following table shows the set of heuristic vectors at each non-terminal node.

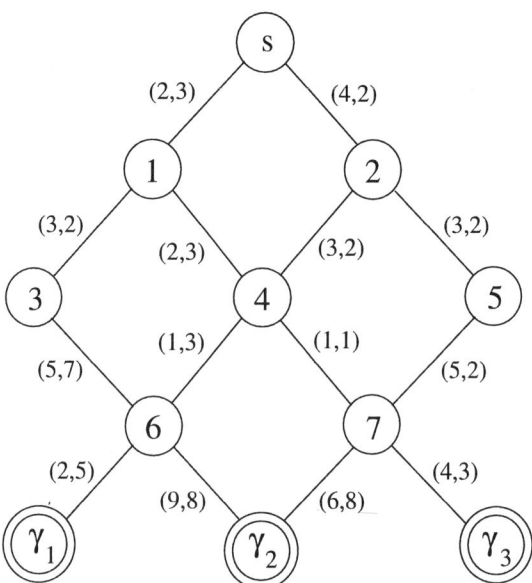

Figure 2.1: A Multiobjective OR-graph

n	$H(n)$
s	(2,3),(4,2)
n_1	(2,3),(3,2)
n_2	(3,2)
n_3	(5,7)
n_4	(1,1)
n_5	(5,2)
n_6	(2,5)
n_7	(4,3)

Algorithm MOA* starts with the node s. Since $G(s)$ is empty, $F(S)$ is the same as $H(s)$. In the first iteration, node s is expanded to generate the successors n_1 and n_2. The cost vectors computed at the nodes are shown in the following table. n' refers to the parent (of n) being expanded.

n	$G(n)$	$F(n)$	n'	LABEL(n',n)
n_1	(2,3)	(4,6),(5,5)	s	(2,3)
n_2	(4,2)	(7,4)	s	(4,2)

Since both n_1 and n_2 have non-dominated cost vectors, they are present in ND. Without loss of generality let us assume that n_1 is selected for expansion. Then n_3 and n_4 will be generated. The following table depicts the cost vectors of the nodes in OPEN.

2.4 Previous Work: Multiobjective A*

n	$G(n)$	$F(n)$	n'	LABEL(n',n)
n_2	(4,2)	(7,4)		
n_3	(5,5)	(10,12)	n_1	(5,5)
n_4	(4,6)	(5,7)	n_1	(4,6)

Now ND consists of nodes n_2 and n_4 only (the cost of n_3 is dominated by the costs of n_2 and n_4). Again without loss of generality, let us assume that n_2 is selected first. Then n_5 will be generated and n_4 will be regenerated.

n	$G(n)$	$F(n)$	n'	LABEL(n',n)
n_3	(5,5)	(10,12)		
n_4	(4,6),(7,4)	(5,7),(8,5)	n_2	(7,4)
n_5	(7,4)	(12,6)	n_2	(7,4)

Since (5,7) dominates (10,12), and (8,5) dominates (12,6), ND now contains only node n_4. When n_4 is expanded, nodes n_6 and n_7 are generated.

n	$G(n)$	$F(n)$	n'	LABEL(n',n)
n_3	(5,5)	(10,12)		
n_5	(7,4)	(12,6)		
n_6	(5,9),(8,7)	(7,14),(10,12)	n_4	(5,9),(8,7)
n_7	(5,7),(8,5)	(9,10),(12,8)	n_4	(5,7),(8,5)

Now ND consists of n_5, n_6 and n_7 (n_3 is dominated by n_7). The node n_6 enters ND by virtue of the non-dominated cost vector (7,14) in $F(n_6)$. Similarly n_7 enters ND by virtue of the cost vector (9,10). Let us assume that n_5 is selected next and n_7 is regenerated. However, since the cost of the new path to n_7, that is (12,6), is dominated by the cost of an existing path, that is (8,5), the regeneration of node n_7 does not affect any cost set.

n	$G(n)$	$F(n)$	n'	LABEL(n',n)
n_3	(5,5)	(10,12)		
n_6	(5,9),(8,7)	(7,14),(10,12)		
n_7	(5,7),(8,5)	(9,10),(12,8)		

Now ND consists of nodes n_6 and n_7. Let us assume that n_7 is expanded first to generate the nodes γ_2 and γ_3.

n	$G(n)$	$F(n)$	n'	LABEL(n',n)
n_3	(5,5)	(10,12)		
n_6	(5,9),(8,7)	(7,14),(10,12)		
γ_2	(11,15),(14,13)	(11,15),(14,13)	n_7	(11,15),(14,13)
γ_3	(9,10),(12,8)	(9,10),(12,8)	n_7	(9,10),(12,8)

Now ND consists of n_6 and γ_3 (the cost vector (9,10) of γ_3 dominates all cost vectors of γ_2 and n_3). Since γ_3 is a goal node it is preferred over n_6. Therefore γ_3 is selected next. This yields two solutions — (9,10) and (12,8). In the next iteration n_6 is selected for expansion. Thus γ_2 is regenerated and γ_1 is generated for the first time. Regeneration of γ_2 does not change any cost set.

n	$G(n)$	$F(n)$	n'	LABEL(n',n)
n_3	(5,5)	(10,12)		
γ_2	(11,15),(14,13)	(11,15),(14,13)		
γ_1	(7,14),(10,12)	(7,14),(10,12)	n_6	(7,14),(10,12)

ND now contains only node γ_1. This yields the non-dominated solution of cost (7,14). Since all nodes in OPEN are now dominated by the existing solution costs, the algorithm terminates with the following set of solutions:

$$\{(7,14),(9,10),(12,8)\}$$

2.5 Conclusion

Based on the algorithm MOA^*, Stewart and White [90, 91] have established several results on multiobjective state space search. They have shown that when the heuristic function is admissible, the algorithm MOA^* terminates with the entire set of non-dominated solutions. Several well known results from the conventional search model have been extended to the multiobjective framework. For example, it has been shown that if A and A' are two versions of MOA^* such that A is at least as informed as A' then A expands no more nodes than A'. They have also established that monotonicity of the multiobjective heuristic function implies admissibility.

The contents of this chapter forms the background of our work on multiobjective heuristic search. In the following chapter we present our results on multiobjective state space search. Chapter 5 presents our contributions on multiobjective problem reduction search, and in chapter 6 we describe an interesting variant of the game tree search problem cast in the multiobjective framework.

Chapter 3

Multiobjective State Space Search

The multiobjective search model appears to be an interesting general framework for solving multicriteria optimization problems. However several practical aspects need to be considered before actually applying the scheme to real world problems. For the conventional search model, extensive work has been done on developing feasible and effective search strategies. Algorithmic improvements on the basic search strategies such as A^* have also been suggested. The effect of different types of heuristics have been investigated to cover a broader spectrum of search problems.

This chapter addresses two broad topics. The first is to study multiobjective state space search under two different types of heuristics, namely non-monotone and inadmissible heuristics. The other is to develop search strategies for the multiobjective framework that operate under space constraints. Most of the analyses in this chapter assumes that the state space is an implicitly specified tree. Extensions to graphs have been considered separately.

In this chapter we generalize the concept of *pathmax* to the multiobjective framework and show that in this model the utility of *pathmax* extends over a wider class of problem instances than in the conventional search model. For the problem of searching with inadmissible heuristics we show that in general only brute force search strategies are guaranteed to find all non-dominated solutions. We also analyze specific conditions under which a best-first search strategy such as MOA^* is admissible.

One of the major contributions of the present work has been to investigate the utility of using an induced total order to guide the selection process. In this chapter we establish several results which show that the policy of using an induced total order called *K-order* is useful in many situations. Using the concepts of *pathmax* and *K-ordering* we present an improved version of the algorithm MOA^*. The new algorithm is called MOA^{**}.

The problem of multiobjective heuristic search in restricted memory has also been considered in this chapter. We show that the main difficulty in extending known memory bounded search techniques from the conventional model arises from the existence of multiple candidate back-up cost vectors in the pruned space. We then establish that if an induced total order such as *K-order* is used to guide the partial order search then it is possible to construct a strategy that backs up a single cost vector while backtracking and yet guarantees admissibility. A linear space search strategy called MOMA*0 is presented on these lines. Several variants of the strategy are suggested to cater to specific situations.

The chapter is organized as follows. Section 3.2 presents the generalization of *pathmax* to the multiobjective search scheme and establishes the related results. The policy of using an induced total order to guide partial order heuristic search is considered in section 3.3. In section 3.4 we use the concepts of *pathmax* and *K-ordering* to develop the strategy MOA^{**}. Section 3.5 addresses the problem of multiobjective state space search in bounded memory. The algorithm $MOMA^*0$ is presented in the same section. In section 3.6 we analyze the problem of multiobjective search using inadmissible heuristics and present related results. Section 3.7 outlines the extension of the search strategies to graphs.

3.1 Preliminary notations and definitions

Most of the notations used in this chapter are standard notations adopted in heuristic search literature. We therefore highlight only the characteristic terminologies of multi-objective heuristic search.

$+$	:	If a and b are vectors (of equal dimension) then $a + b$ denotes the vector formed by summing a and b in each individual dimension.
$-$	:	If a and b are vectors (of equal dimension) then $a - b$ denotes the vector formed by subtracting b from a in each individual dimension.
$vmax(a,b)$	:	If a and b are vectors (of equal dimension) then $vmax(a,b)$ denotes a vector which is equal to the maximum of a and b in each individual dimension.
H(n)	:	The non-dominated set of heuristic vectors computed at node n.
G(n)	:	If the search space is a tree then $G(n)$ is the vector valued cost of the path from the start node s to node n. If the search space is a graph then $G(n)$ denotes the non-dominated set of vector valued path costs from s to n in the current explicit search graph.
F(n)	:	The non-dominated set of cost vectors of node n computed as $h(n) + g(n)$, where $h(n) \in H(n)$ and $g(n) \in G(n)$. In the case of trees $g(n)$ is the same as $G(n)$.

The definition of *dominance* is given in chapter 2 (Def 2.1). The definition of admissible and non-monotonic heuristics are as follows.

Def # 3.1 Admissible heuristics:
A multiobjective heuristic function is said to be admissible if the set $H(n)$ of heuristic vectors computed at each node n satisfies the following property:

Admissibility property: For every solution path $P(s, \gamma)$ through node n (where s is the start node and γ is any goal node), there exists a heuristic vector $h(n)$ in $H(n)$ such that $h(n)$ either dominates the cost vector of the solution path from n to γ or is equal to it.

It should be noted that in one extreme case $H(n)$ may contain only a single vector which satisfies the above property, while in the other extreme case $H(n)$ may contain a distinct vector corresponding to each solution path through node n. □

Def # 3.2 Monotone heuristics:
A multiobjective heuristic function is said be monotone (or consistent) if for all nodes n_i and n_j, such that n_j is a successor of n_i, the set $H(n_i)$ of heuristic vectors computed at node n_i satisfies the following property:

Monotonicity property: For each heuristic vector $h(n_j)$ in $H(n_j)$, there exists a heuristic $h(n_i)$ in $H(n_i)$, such that $h(n_i)$ either dominates the vector $c(n_i, n_j) + h(n_j)$ or is equal to it. $c(n_i, n_j)$ denotes the cost vector of the edge from n_i to n_j.

□

3.2 Multidimensional Pathmax

Pathmax is a standard concept in heuristic search which is used to strengthen admissible non-monotonic heuristics during search. The basic idea is to use the cumulative heuristic information available along the search path to compute the heuristic cost of a node, so that the heuristic cost of the node is consistent with the heuristic cost of its ancestors. We illustrate the idea of *pathmax* through the following example from the conventional search model.

Example # 3.1 Consider the tree shown in Fig 3.1. Since $h(s)$ is 11 and the heuristics are admissible, the cost of every solution path must be at least 11. It follows that the heuristic cost of node n_1 must be at least 7. Thus the heuristic cost 0 evaluated at node n_1 is inconsistent with the heuristic cost of s and should be replaced by the stronger estimate 7.

Instead of using the evaluation function $f(n) = g(n) + h(n)$, the *pathmax* technique uses the following evaluation function:

$$f(n) = max\left\{g(n') + h(n') \mid n' \text{ is on the current path to } n\right\}$$

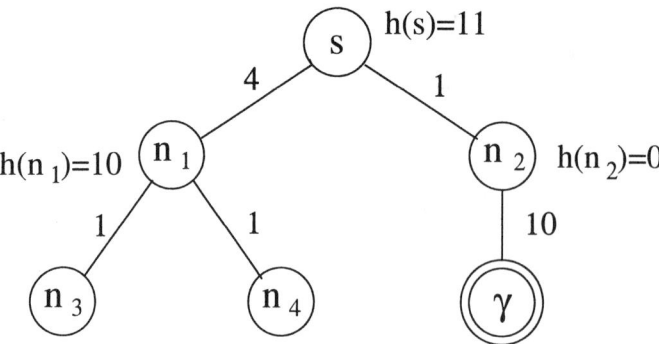

Figure 3.1: Tree illustrating the advantage of *pathmax*

The improvement on best-first algorithms like A^* by virtue of *pathmax* is evident from Fig 3.1. Using *pathmax* $f(n_1) = f(n_2) = 11$. If A^* resolves the tie between n_1 and n_2 by comparing $g(n_1)$ and $g(n_2)$, it will expand n_2 and generate γ of cost 11. In the next iteration it will select γ (since it is a goal node) and terminate. Node n_1 will not be expanded. On the other hand, if *pathmax* is not used then $f(n_1) = 4$, and therefore n_1 will be expanded. □

The idea of using *pathmax* to propagate the cost of the parent node to the child node was suggested by Mero [66]. *Pathmax* has been found to be useful on the following accounts.

- Dechter and Pearl [25] and Gelperin [31] have shown that by using *pathmax* it is possible to develop A^*-like algorithms that are superior to A^* in terms of the set of nodes expanded. However they have also shown that such extensions of A^* may expand a smaller set of nodes only in *pathological* problem instances, that is, in problem instances where *every* solution path contains at least one fully informed non-goal node. It has been shown [25] that in non-pathological cases the same set of nodes will be expanded irrespective of using *pathmax*.

- Martelli [61], and Bagchi and Mahanti [1] have shown that it may be possible to the reduce the number of nodes re-expanded by A^* in graph search problems considerably if a strategy similar to *pathmax* is used. Chakrabarti et al [10] have also used this result in memory bounded search.

Therefore in the conventional search model, the utility of *pathmax* in *tree* search is limited to *pathological* problem instances only. In the case of graphs *pathmax* may be used to reduce the number of node re-expansions in non-pathological cases as well. However the *set* of nodes expanded remain the same irrespective of using *pathmax*.

In this section, we generalize the concept of *pathmax* to the multiobjective search model. We shall show that in the multiobjective search framework *pathmax* may reduce

3.2 Multidimensional Pathmax

the set of nodes expanded even in non-pathological cases [1].

3.2.1 The definition of *pathmax*

When the successor m of node n is generated, each heuristic vector $h(m)$ evaluated by the heuristic function at node m is updated using *pathmax* as follows:

> For each vector $h(n)$ in $H(n)$
> For each vector $h(m)$ evaluated at node m
> 1. Create a new vector $h'(m)$ as follows:
> $$h'(m) \leftarrow vmax\{h(m), h(n) - c(n,m)\}$$
> where $c(n,m)$ denotes the cost vector of the edge (n,m), and the function *vmax* is as defined in section 3.1.
> 2. Put $h'(m)$ in H(m) and remove dominated vectors from H(m), if any.

Thus *pathmax* is used in the same way as in the single objective search model, but for every heuristic vector and along each dimension of the vector.

3.2.2 Two basic properties of *pathmax*

In order to establish the validity of multidimensional *pathmax* in the multiobjective framework we prove the following two basic properties. The proofs consider trees only.

Theorem # 3.1 *The set of heuristics remain admissible if pathmax is used in MOA*.*
Proof: We first prove that if the set of heuristics at a node n is admissible then the set of admissible heuristics at each immediate successor node m remains admissible when *pathmax* is used.

If the set of heuristics at node n is admissible, then corresponding to every solution path to a goal node γ through node n, there exists $h(n)$ in $H(n)$ such that $h(n)$ either dominates $h^*(n,\gamma)$ or is equal to it, where $h^*(n,\gamma)$ denotes the cost vector of the path from n to γ. If the same solution path contains node m then $h(n) - c(n,m)$ either dominates or is equal to $h^*(m,\gamma)$. Now since $h(m)$ is admissible, it follows that $h(m)$ also dominates $h^*(m,\gamma)$ or is equal to it. Therefore, the heuristic vector $h'(m)$ computed using *pathmax* as follows will also dominate $h^*(m,\gamma)$:
$$h'(m) \leftarrow vmax\{h(m), h(n) - c(n,m)\}$$
Thus H(m) either contains $h'(m)$ or some vector which dominates $h'(m)$. It follows that the set of heuristics $H(m)$ computed using *pathmax* is admissible.

We have shown that the set of heuristics at a node remain admissible provided the set of heuristics at its parent node is admissible. Since the set of heuristics at the start node remain the same, the result follows by induction. □

---

[1] Reprinted from *Information Processing Letters*, 55, Dasgupta, Chakrabarti, DeSarkar, *Utility of pathmax in partial order heuristic search*, 317-322, 1995, with permisssion from Elsevier Science.

Theorem # 3.2 *Every node expanded by MOA* using pathmax is also expanded by MOA* without pathmax in the worst case.*

Proof: Each heuristic vector computed at a node without pathmax either equals or dominates some heuristic vector computed using *pathmax*. Therefore if a node and its ancestors have one or more cost vectors that are non-dominated when computed using pathmax, then the node and its ancestors are non-dominated if pathmax is not used. Since MOA* explores all non-dominated cost paths in the worst case, the result follows. It may be noted however that for certain individual instances anomalies may occur due to tie resolutions where the worst case set of nodes is not expanded. □

3.2.3 The significance of *pathmax*

We now establish the result that in the multiobjective search framework *pathmax* may be used to reduce the *set* of nodes expanded by MOA^* in non-pathological problem instances as well.

Theorem # 3.3 *There exists non-pathological problem instances (that is, problem instances in which not all solution paths contain a fully informed non-goal node) where MOA* will have to expand an arbitrarily large number of nodes which will not be expanded if* pathmax *is used.*

Proof: Consider the tree in Fig 3.2. The cost vector of each edge is shown beside the edge. The heuristic vectors computed without pathmax are shown beside the nodes. For simplicity, we consider only 2-dimensional costs and only one heuristic vector per node. It should be noted that no non-goal node along the solution path to node n_4 is totally informed (in either dimension).

When n_1 is expanded by MOA*, the heuristic vector (1,13) is computed at node n_3 and $c(n_1, n_3)$ is found to be (1,1). From this $F(n_3)$ is computed as (2,14). Likewise $F(n_2)$ is computed as (2,10). Since (2,10) dominates (2,14), n_2 will be expanded earlier than n_3 to generate n_4. Then $F(n_4)$ is computed as (3,12). Now either n_4 or n_3 may be selected. Irrespective of which is selected earlier, the expansion of n_3 is certain. If $H(n_5)$ is computed without *pathmax*, then $F(n_5) = (4,9)$, and the expansion of n_5 is also certain since (4,9) is non-dominated by the cost (3,12) of node n_4. On the other hand, using *pathmax* $H(n_5)$ is computed as (2,12). Therefore $F(n_5)$ becomes (4,14) which is dominated by the cost (3,12) of n_4. Thus n_4 will be selected earlier and the solution of cost (3,12) will be obtained. It follows that n_5 will never be expanded.

It is easy to see that the expansion of node n_5 may lead to the expansion of an arbitrarily large number of nodes in the subtree rooted at node n_5, each of which contains some heuristic vector non-dominated by (3,12) without *pathmax*. The result follows. □

3.3 An induced total ordering: *K-ordering*

Efficiency of problem solving in the multiobjective search framework is largely dependent on effective partial order search strategies for finding the set of non-dominated solutions.

3.3 An induced total ordering: K-ordering

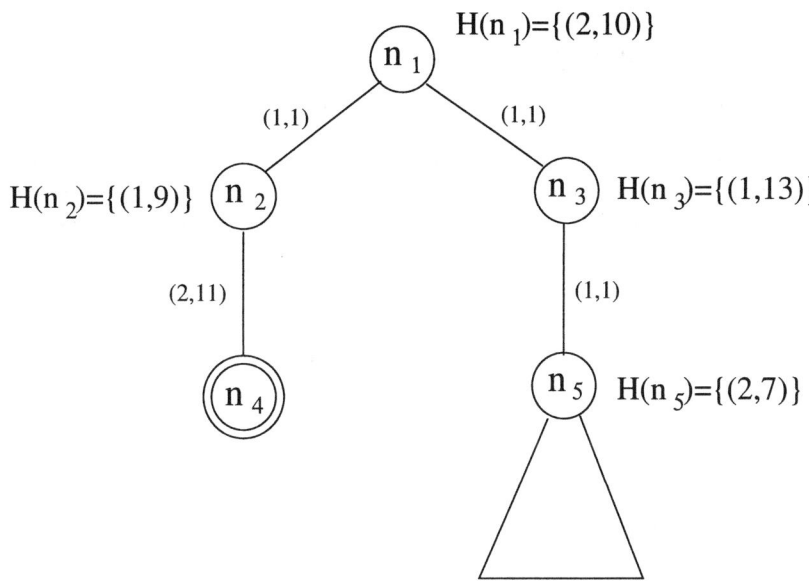

Figure 3.2: Multiobjective graph illustrating the advantage of *pathmax*

A characteristic feature of partial order search is the presence of multiple non-inferior search paths each of which must be explored in order to guarantee admissibility. The set of nodes in OPEN that have one or more non-dominated cost vectors represent these non-inferior search paths and therefore must be expanded by admissible search strategies like MOA*. We formally define non-dominated nodes in OPEN as follows:

Def # 3.3 Non-dominated node:
A node n in OPEN is said to be non-dominated if at least one of the cost vectors in $F(n)$ is non-dominated by all cost vectors of every other node in OPEN and the cost vector of all solution nodes found so far.

It may be easily shown that the order in which the non-dominated nodes in OPEN are selected does not affect the total number of nodes expanded by a strategy like MOA* in the worst case. We shall present a proof of this result later in this chapter. In this section we introduce the policy of using an induced total order to select a non-dominated node from OPEN. While this policy does not affect the number of nodes expanded by strategies such as MOA*, we shall show that there are several other benefits of using the policy.

A basic advantage of using an induced total ordering is that we then have a mechanism of identifying a non-dominated node from OPEN without having to identify the entire set of non-dominated nodes in OPEN. This is easily possible if the induced total order is defined in the following manner.

Def # 3.4 K-ordering:
Let y^1 and y^2 be two K-dimensional vectors. Then, based on K-ordering, $y^1 > y^2$ if

$$\exists j,\ 1 \leq j \leq K \text{ such that } y_j^1 > y_j^2 \text{ and } \forall i, i < j,\ y_i^1 = y_i^2$$

It essentially represents the policy of comparing two vector-valued costs on the basis of the first component; breaking ties on the basis of the second component; breaking further ties on the basis of the third component, and so on. The other relational operators (such as $=$ and $<$) are defined in a likewise manner.

The basic idea is derived from the single objective search strategies where the data structure OPEN is ordered on the basis of the costs of the nodes. It is easy to see that the minimum cost vector in *K-order* is always non-dominated in a set of cost vectors. Since a node may have several cost vectors (in $F(n)$), we define the *representative cost vector* of a node based on the induced total order as follows.

Def # 3.5 The representative cost vector of a node:
The representative cost vector of node n is the minimum cost vector using K-ordering on the set of cost vectors $F(n)$ which is non-dominated by the cost vector of every solution found earlier.

If the representative cost vector of a node becomes dominated by the cost vector of some solution found during the course of the search, then the next non-dominated cost (in K-order) becomes the current representative cost of the node. The representative cost vector of a path in the state space is the same as the representative cost vector of its tip node.

In this chapter, we shall show that using an induced total ordering such as *K-ordering* to guide the partial order search may be useful in several situations. The main results are as follows:

- In section 3.4, we show that if *K-ordering* is used to guide the search, then in some cases it may not be necessary to evaluate all the heuristic vectors at a node. This result is particularly useful in problems where generating the heuristics are costly. We consider one such problem in chapter 4.

- In section 3.4, we also observe that in two-objective problems (which are quite numerous) we can simplify the process of dominance checking by using *K-ordering* to guide the search.

- In section 3.5, we discuss the advantage of using *K-ordering* in memory bounded search. In particular, we show that though the space pruned by a memory bounded search strategy (while backtracking) may contain a large number of nodes having one or more non-dominated cost vectors, it is possible to back up a single cost vector from the pruned space and yet guarantee admissibility by using *K-ordering* to guide the search.

3.4 The algorithm MOA**

By using the ideas of *K-ordering* and *pathmax*, we now present a modified version of the algorithm MOA*, which we shall call MOA**. Since the new algorithm utilizes the path information through *pathmax*, it follows from the properties of *pathmax* that the new algorithm will be superior to MOA* in terms of the worst case number of nodes expanded. In this section we also discuss the advantages of using *K-ordering* in the new algorithm. In this section we present the algorithm MOA** for trees. The extension of the algorithm to graphs have been presented in section 3.7.

3.4.1 The Algorithm Outline

The algorithm outline (for trees) is given below. The set of heuristic vectors at node n is denoted by $H(n)$ and the set of cost vectors of node n is denoted by $F(n)$. If any dimension of a cost vector in $F(n)$ is infinity, it would signify that the cost vector is useless, since it does not underestimate the cost of any finite solution. If all the cost vectors of a node are infinity, then the node can be discarded altogether.

Algorithm MOA^{**}

1. **[INITIALIZE]**
    OPEN $\leftarrow$ s ; SOLUTION_GOALS $\leftarrow \phi$; SOLUTION_COSTS $\leftarrow \phi$;

2. **[TERMINATE]**
    If OPEN is empty then
        2.1 Output the solutions from SOLUTION_GOALS.
        2.2 Terminate.

3. **[SELECT]**
    3.1 Remove the node n in OPEN with the minimum representative cost vector in K-order. Let this cost vector be f(n). Resolve ties in favor of goal nodes, else arbitrarily.

4. **[DOMINANCE CHECK]**
    If the representative cost vector of node n is dominated by the cost vector of a solution in SOLUTION_COSTS then:
    4.1 Remove f(n) from F(n).
    4.2 Select the next non-dominated cost vector of n (in K-order).
        4.2.1 If there is no non-dominated cost vector in $F(n)$ then
            4.2.1.1 Discard node n.
            4.2.1.2 Goto [Step 2].
        4.2.2 Otherwise declare the new vector as the representative cost of n
            4.2.2.1 Return node n to OPEN.
            4.2.2.2 Goto [Step 3].

5. **[IDENTIFY SOLUTIONS]**
    If n is a goal node then
    5.1 Put n in SOLUTION_GOALS and its cost vector in SOLUTION_COSTS.
    5.2 Goto [Step 2].

6. **[EXPAND]**
    Expand n and examine its successors.
    6.1 Generate the successors of n.
    6.2 If n has no successors, Goto [Step 2].
    6.3 Otherwise, for each successor n_j of n, do the following:
        6.3.1 Evaluate the non-dominated set of heuristics $H(n_j)$ using *pathmax*.
        6.3.2 Compute the set $F(n_j)$ by adding the cost vectors in $H(n_j)$ with $G(n_j)$.
        6.3.3 Determine the minimum cost vector in $F(n_j)$ using K-ordering.
            Declare that cost as the representative cost vector of n_j.
        6.3.4 Enter n_j in OPEN.

7. **[ITERATE]**
    Goto [step 2]

It should be noted that unlike MOA*, the algorithm MOA** tests whether the cost of a node is dominated by a solution cost *after* the node has been selected. Thus, if it is found that all costs of a node are dominated, then MOA** can discard it altogether.

3.4.2 Admissibility & Optimality

This section deals with the admissibility and optimality issues of MOA**. The properties of MOA** are very much similar to those of the algorithm A* in the conventional search domain. Similar properties were proved for the algorithm MOA* by Stewart and White [91]. The objective of this section is to establish the correctness of MOA^{**} and highlight some of the other properties of the algorithm. The following assumptions define the domain in which MOA^{**} is admissible.

Assumption # 3.1 *The heuristic function is admissible.*

Assumption # 3.2 *The number of children of a node are finite.*

Assumption # 3.3 *All non-dominated solutions are of finite length and have finite cost vectors, and the cost vectors of infinite paths are dominated by solutions.*

The following two theorems establish the admissibility of MOA^{**}.

3.4 The algorithm MOA**

Theorem # 3.4 *If there exists a goal node γ in the search space, then MOA** is guaranteed to terminate.*
Proof : We first show that paths are expanded only up to a finite depth. Let us consider a node n at infinite depth. By assumption 3.3, each of its cost vectors is dominated by the cost vector of every solution path. Since the cost vector of the path $P(s,\gamma)$ is finite, the cost vector of γ and some cost vector of every ancestor of γ dominate every cost vector of node n. Until γ is selected either γ or one of its ancestors must be present in OPEN. Since MOA** selects only those nodes that are non-dominated in OPEN and non-dominated by SOLUTION_COSTS, it follows that the node n at infinite depth will never be expanded.

The number of successors of a node are finite (by assumption 3.2), which also implies that the number of paths up to a finite depth are finite. Since a finite set of paths are expanded up to a finite depth, the termination of MOA** is guaranteed. $\square$

Theorem # 3.5 *MOA** is admissible, that is, it terminates with all non-dominated solutions in the entire search space.*
Proof: When the heuristics are admissible, every ancestor node of a non-dominated solution node will contain a cost vector that either dominates or is equal to the cost vector of the solution node. It follows that every ancestor of a non-dominated goal node is also non-dominated. Therefore, until the solution node is found OPEN will contain a non-dominated node and MOA** cannot terminate. Since termination is guaranteed by theorem 3.4 the result follows. $\square$

In this context it must be noted that the admissibility of MOA** is subject to the admissibility of the heuristic function, that is, each ancestor node of a goal contains at least one cost vector which dominates the cost vector of the solution. If there exists a non-dominated solution γ in the search space such that some node n in the path from s to γ does not have a cost vector which dominates the cost of γ, then MOA** is not guaranteed to find the solution γ. This happens when all the cost vectors of node n are dominated and node n is discarded by MOA**. In order to guarantee that all non-dominated solutions are found under such situations, an algorithm will have to expand dominated nodes as well. This indicates that brute-force search strategies may be the only strategies that are guaranteed to find all non-dominated solutions. However, it is easy to see that under such circumstances MOA** is guaranteed to find all those goals whose ancestors have admissible heuristics.

We now show that the set of nodes expanded by MOA** does not depend on the way in which the induced total ordering is defined. In other words we show that instead of using *K-ordering* if the non-dominated nodes are selected from OPEN in any other order, the total number of nodes expanded by MOA** in the worst case remains the same.

Theorem # 3.6 *A node n is expanded by MOA** only if n and all its ancestors have one or more cost vectors that are either equal to or non-dominated by the cost vector of every solution node in the search space. If the node n and its ancestors also have at least one cost vector that is non-dominated by the cost vectors of every solution path not containing n, then the node n will definitely be expanded by MOA**.*
Proof: We prove the sufficiency condition first. If a node n and all its ancestors have one or

more non-dominated cost vectors then step 2 of MOA** shows that the node is a candidate for expansion. However, if every non-dominated cost vector of n (or of one of its ancestors) equals the cost vector of other solution paths, then it is possible that those solution paths are found earlier and n is never expanded. Otherwise, it is easy to see that the node n will be expanded by MOA**.

Now let us consider a node n selected for expansion in [step 3] of MOA**. It is expanded if its representative cost vector is non-dominated by every solution node found so far. Let us assume that this cost vector is dominated by the cost vector of some non-dominated goal node γ in the search space which has not been found so far. This leads us to a contradiction because until γ is found, OPEN will contain either γ or one of its ancestors, each of which has one or more cost vectors that dominate the cost vector of γ (and therefore dominate the representative cost vector of n). The result follows by induction on the ancestors of n. □

Based on theorem 3.6, we define the nodes that are *surely expanded* by MOA** as follows.

Def # 3.6 Surely expanded nodes:
*If a node n and each of its ancestors have one or more cost vectors that are non-dominated by every solution path which does not contain n, then n is **surely expanded** by MOA**.*

Since theorem 3.6 establishes the fact that the set of *surely expanded nodes* will have to be expanded by any admissible strategy irrespective of the order of selection of non-dominated nodes from OPEN, it follows that in the worst case, the set of nodes *surely expanded* by MOA^* and MOA^{**} are the same. Thus the optimality results proved by Stewart and White [91] for MOA^* extends to MOA^{**} as well.

We now establish a property of MOA^{**} which will be useful in describing the advantage of using *K-ordering* in partial order search.

Theorem # 3.7 *The non-dominated solution nodes are found by MOA** in strictly increasing K-ordered sequence of their cost vectors.*
Proof: Let γ_1 and γ_2 be two non-dominated solutions in the search space such that the cost vector of γ_1 is less than the cost vector of γ_2 in K-order but γ_2 is found by MOA** before γ_1. This means that when γ_2 was selected from OPEN, there were no node in OPEN having one or more cost vectors that dominate the cost of γ_1 because then that node would have had a smaller representative cost vector. This leads us to a contradiction because OPEN must contain either γ_1 or one of its ancestors which (by assumption 3.1) will contain a cost vector that dominates the cost vector of γ_1. □

Based on the results presented so far, the following advantages of using *K-ordering* becomes apparent.

A. Dominance checking in two-objective cases: Since the solution nodes are found in a *K-ordered* sequence of their cost vectors, the list SOLUTION_COSTS is automatically sorted in the first component. In two-objective problems (which are found to occur frequently) the task of testing a cost vector for dominance by solutions can be done in constant time simply by comparing the second dimension of the vector with the second dimension of the latest solution cost vector in SOLUTION_COSTS.

B. **Computing all heuristic vectors is not necessary:** If the heuristic function can generate the heuristic cost vectors of a node in K-order then we may adopt the policy of computing only the representative cost vector of the node at the time of its generation rather than computing the entire set. Since the node may be expanded by virtue of this representative cost vector we save the computational effort of generating the other heuristic vectors of the node. Such an example will be discussed in chapter 4.

The above advantages of using *K-ordering* can easily be generalized to any induced total order on partial order heuristic search. In the next section we shall illustrate the advantage of using *K-ordering* in memory bounded partial order search and show that in the general situation the use of *K-ordering* is a key to perform the search efficiently within given memory constraints.

3.5 Memory bounded multiobjective search

The exorbitant space requirements of search strategies such as A^* have motivated researchers to develop schemes for searching within memory constraints. In the past decade several memory bounded heuristic search strategies have been developed for the general search model. The linear space iterative deepening algorithm IDA* of Korf [48] is one of the foremost among such strategies. The algorithm MA* of Chakrabarti *et al* [10] uses the given memory to retain the *best* portion of the state space and thereby reduce the number of node re-expansions. The algorithm IDA*_CR of Sarkar *et al* [83, 82] and the algorithm DFS* of Rao, Kumar and Korf [79] use suitable techniques to determine the cost cut-off of the next iteration in a way so as to reduce the number of node re-expansions. Other important contributions in the area of restricted memory search include the strategies MREC of Sen and Bagchi [87], IE and SMA* of Russel [81], RBFS of Korf [51, 50] and IDA*_CRM of Sarkar *et al* [84].

In this section we show that the main difficulty in extending standard memory bounded search techniques from the general search model to the multiobjective search model lies in the cost back-up mechanism. We further show that the policy of using *K-ordering* can resolve this problem. This fact is established by incorporating *K-ordering* in a multiobjective search algorithm and showing that the algorithm is admissible and operates in linear space.

3.5.1 Cost back-up and K-ordering

A standard feature of all asymptotically optimal memory bounded search strategies is the act of backing up of costs while backtracking. When such algorithms backtrack from the current path to select a better path, they typically back up the cost of the current path before pruning it, so that the same path is selected only if all other paths of lower cost have been visited. Thus before removing a portion of the explicit search space from the memory the algorithm ensures that the *best* cost from the pruned space is backed up.

Whereas in the conventional search model it is possible to identify a single undisputed *best* cost from the pruned space by using the total order on the cost structure, the same is not possible in the multiobjective model due to the partial order on the cost vectors which allows the existence of multiple non-dominated cost vectors in the pruned space. Since the number of such vectors may be quite large, in general it will not be possible to back-up the entire set of non-dominated vectors due to space limitations. Therefore it is necessary to adopt some technique so that not many cost vectors need to be backed up and yet admissibility is guaranteed. We show that the policy of using an induced total ordering (such as K-ordering) to decide the direction of the search is one such technique to resolve the problem.

In the following sub-sections we shall show that if the policy of searching in a K-ordered best-first manner is adopted then it is possible to back-up only a single cost vector from the pruned space while backtracking. In order to implement this policy over the entire search mechanism (which includes the task of updating the cost vectors of regenerated nodes from the backed up cost vectors) we define a function called *Minf* which assigns updated cost vectors to all nodes in the explicit search space and ensures that the search proceeds in a K-ordered best-first manner.

Once the policy of using K-ordering is adopted, it becomes possible to extend standard memory bounded search techniques to the multiobjective search framework. We present a linear space algorithm called MOMA*0 which incorporates the idea of *K-ordering* with standard memory bounded search techniques.

In this context it must be noted that the admissibility of MOMA*0 only establishes the result that it is *possible* to guarantee admissibility by backing up a single cost vector. While this result guarantees the feasibility of MOMA*0 under all situations it does not necessarily imply that the policy of backing up more than one cost vector from the pruned space is inferior to the policy of backing up a single cost vector. In fact, when sufficient memory is available, the policy of backing up more than one cost vector can typically reduce the number of node re-expansions during search. Thus there is a scope for trade-off between the number of costs to be backed up and the advantage gained due to reduction in the number of node re-expansions. These issues are considered in section 3.5.4 where a variant of the proposed algorithm is suggested that backs up more than one cost vector from the pruned space while backtracking. The performance of these schemes are empirically studied on some practical problems in chapter 4.

3.5 Memory bounded multiobjective search

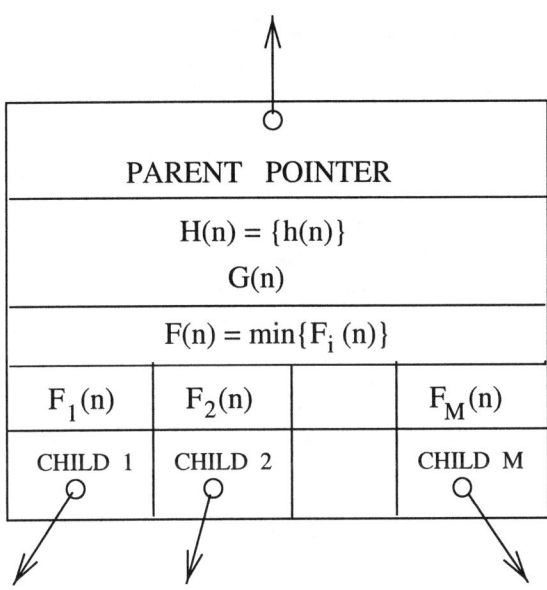

Figure 3.3: The structure of a node

3.5.2 General philosophy of MOMA*0

The algorithm MOMA*0 is a generalization of restricted memory heuristic search techniques (in the conventional search model) with suitable features incorporated to adapt it to the multiobjective framework. In this section we describe the general structure of the nodes and the basic features of the algorithm. In the following discussion we loosely use the term *"minimum"* to refer to *"minimum in K-order"*. Also when we say that a cost vector is *greater* or *less* than another vector we mean that the comparison is on the basis of K-order.

The structure of a node is shown in Fig 3.3. H(n) denotes the set of heuristic vectors of node n using *pathmax*. Each node n maintains a list $\{F_1(n), F_2(n), \ldots, F_M(n)\}$ of cost vectors, where M denotes the number of successors of n and $F_i(n)$ denotes the minimum of the estimated cost vectors of solution paths through node n and its ith child. $F(n)$ denotes the minimum of $\{F_i(n)\}$ and represents the minimum estimated cost vector of solution paths through n. $F(n)$ is called the *representative cost vector* of node n.

The basic features of the algorithm MOMA*0 are as follows.

Use of GL: Algorithm MOMA*0 uses a vector called GL (greatest lower bound), which holds the cost vector of the current *best* path. When a new path is selected, GL denotes the estimated promise of the path.

Use of NEXT_MIN: When MOMA*0 extends the most promising path, it maintains the *next best promise* in a vector called NEXT_MIN. The selected path is extended until its cost vector exceeds the cost vector stored as NEXT_MIN. When this happens, MOMA*0 backtracks up to the node where the cost vector in NEXT_MIN is backed up.

Cost back-up: When MOMA*0 backtracks it backs up *only the minimum (in K-order) of the cost vectors in the current path.*

Backtracking and Cost Revision: If the cost vector of the current search path exceeds GL, and there exists a better alternative path having one or more cost vectors that are less than the cost vector of the current path then MOMA*0 backtracks as follows.

> Let p be the tip node of the current path. Let q be the parent of p and p be its jth child. The value of F(p) is backed up in $F_j(q)$ and F(q) is revised to the minimum among all vectors $F_i(q)$ backed up at q. If this revision alters the vector F(q), then F(q) is backed up to its parent, and so on until either for some node n in the path F(n) is unaltered, or the root node is reached.

We refer to this process of backing up of cost vectors as *cost revision*.

Use of Minf: When a node n is expanded to generate its children m_i, the set of cost vectors of m_i is computed by adding $G(m_i)$ with the heuristic vectors in $H(m_i)$. However, in the cases where m_i is being re-generated $F(m_i)$ should be assigned a cost vector that is consistent with the cost vector that was backed up previously as $F_i(n)$. This assignment is done by a function *Minf* which takes two aspects into account.

1. $F(m_i)$ must be assigned a value greater than or equal to $F_i(n)$.
2. The value assigned to $F(m_i)$ must be consistent with the cost vectors computed at node m_i, that is, it must be dominated by at least one cost vector of node m_i.

The function *Minf* determines *the minimum vector which is greater than or equal to $F_i(n)$ and which is dominated by at least one of the cost vectors of m_i* and assigns this vector to $F(m_i)$.

Test for dominance: If the vector F(m) of node m is dominated by the cost vector of some solution found previously, then the dominated heuristic vectors in H(m) are removed. If H(m) becomes empty, then the $F(m)$ is set to infinity, and the algorithm backtracks. Otherwise, F(m) is assigned a new vector by applying *Minf* on $F_i(n)$ and the new $H(m)$, where n is the parent of m, and m is the ith successor of n.

Since the search proceeds in K-order, it is easy to see that the first dimension of the representative cost vector of a node is greater than or equal to the first dimension of the cost vector of every solution found so far. Therefore, while testing for dominance against the cost vector of a solution, we ignore the first dimension.

3.5 Memory bounded multiobjective search

Termination condition: When a non-dominated solution node is found its path to the source is traced and the cost vector of the path is saved. Then the cost vector of the node is set to infinity, so that the algorithm backtracks and proceeds along alternative paths for other solutions. When all the cost vectors of a path becomes dominated by the cost vectors of solutions, infinity is backed up along that path. The algorithm terminates, when infinity is backed up along all paths.

3.5.3 Algorithm $MOMA^*0$

The outline of the algorithm in recursive form is given below. The *min* operator refers to the minimum in K-order.

MOMA*0(node:n,cost:GL,cost:NEXT_MIN)

1. If $F(n) > GL$ return $F(n)$

2. Test for dominated heuristics
    2.1 Remove all dominated heuristics in H(n)
    2.2 If H(n) is empty, return ∞
    2.3 Recalculate $F(n) \leftarrow Minf(GL, G(n), H(n))$
    2.4 If F(n) increases then return F(n)

3. IF n is a goal node THEN
    3.1 Put n in SOLUTION_GOALS and its cost in SOLUTION_COSTS
    3.2 Output the solution path and return ∞

4. Expand n, generating all its successors.
    4.1 For each successor m_i of n
        4.1.1 Evaluate the set $H(m_i)$ of non-dominated heuristics
        4.1.3 Calculate $G(m_i) \leftarrow G(n) + c(n, m_i)$
            where $c(n, m_i)$ is the cost of the arc (n, m_i).
        4.1.4 Use the function Minf to evaluate the value of $F(m_i)$
        4.1.5 Set $F_i(m_i) \leftarrow F(m_i) \; \forall i$
        4.1.6 Set $F_i(n) \leftarrow F(m_i)$
    4.2 Set $F' \leftarrow min\{F_i(n), \forall i\}$.

5. Let m_j be the successor with cost F'. Set $F'' \leftarrow min\{F_i(n), \forall i, i \neq j\}$.
    5.1 $F_j(n) \leftarrow MOMA^*0(m_j, GL, min(NEXT\_MIN, F''))$
    5.2 Set $F' \leftarrow min\{F_i(n), \forall i\}$.
    5.3 Set $MIN \leftarrow min(NEXT\_MIN, F')$
    5.4 If $F' = MIN$ THEN
        5.4.1 Set $GL \leftarrow NEXT\_MIN$
        5.4.2 Goto [Step 5]
    Else return F'

The function: *Minf*

Whenever the ith successor m of node n is generated, $F(m)$ is assigned *the minimum vector which is greater than or equal to $F_i(n)$ and which is dominated by at least one of the cost vectors of m*. The outline of the function is given below:

$Minf(F_i(n), G(m), H(m))$
    Let $f_j(n)$ denote the jth dimension of $F_i(n)$.
    1. Construct a set $\hat{F}(m)$ in the following way:
        1.1 For each heuristic $h(m) \in H(m)$ create a new vector $f(m)$:
            1.1.1 $f(m) \leftarrow G(m) + h(m)$
                Let $f_j(m)$ denote the jth dimension of $f(m)$.
            1.1.2 For $j = 1$ to $j = K$
                If $f_j(n) \geq f_j(m)$ Then Set $f_j(m) \leftarrow f_j(n)$
                Else Goto [Step 1.1.3]
            1.1.3 Put $f(m)$ in $\hat{F}(m)$
    2. Return the minimum vector (in K-order) from $\hat{F}(m)$.
End.

The following example illustrates the working of the algorithm $MOMA^*0$ and justifies the use of the function *Minf*. To demonstrate the basic idea we consider a simple case where each node has a single cost vector.

Example # 3.2 We show the operation of MOMA*0 on the graph of Fig 3.4. Since H(s) is (3,2,2), the algorithm starts with GL as (3,2,2).

n	$F(n)$	$F_1(n)$	$F_2(n)$
s	(3,2,2)	(3,2,2)	(3,2,2)
GL = (3,2,2)		NEXT_MIN = (∞, ∞, ∞)	

At first node s is expanded to generate nodes n_1 and n_2.

n	$F(n)$	$F_1(n)$	$F_2(n)$
s	(4,3,4)	(4,3,4)	(10,10,10)
n_1	(4,3,4)	(4,3,4)	(4,3,4)
n_2	(10,10,10)	(10,10,10)	(10,10,10)
GL = (4,3,4)		NEXT_MIN = (10,10,10)	

Since $F(n_1)$ is less than $F(n_2)$, node n_1 is selected. n_1 is expanded to generate nodes n_3 and n_8.

3.5 Memory bounded multiobjective search

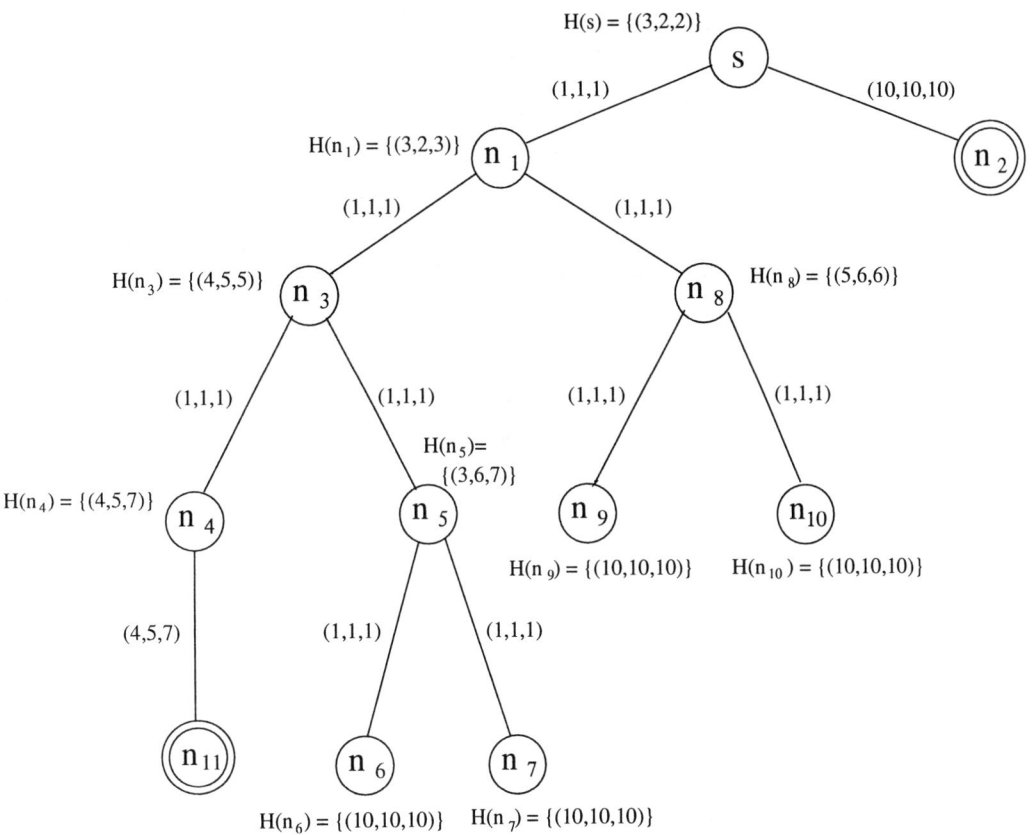

Figure 3.4: Graph illustrating the utility of *Minf*

n	$F(n)$	$F_1(n)$	$F_2(n)$
s	(4,3,4)	(4,3,4)	(10,10,10)
n_1	(6,7,7)	(6,7,7)	(7,8,8)
n_2	(10,10,10)	(10,10,10)	(10,10,10)
n_3	(6,7,7)	(6,7,7)	(6,7,7)
n_8	(7,8,8)	(7,8,8)	(7,8,8)
GL = (6,7,7)		NEXT_MIN = (7,8,8)	

Though the cost vector of the path has exceeded the previous value of GL it is still less than any other alternative. Therefore the value of GL becomes (6,7,7). In the next iteration n_3 is selected and expanded to generate nodes n_4 and n_5.

n	$F(n)$	$F_1(n)$	$F_2(n)$
s	(4,3,4)	(4,3,4)	(10,10,10)
n_1	(6,7,7)	(6,7,7)	(7,8,8)
n_2	(10,10,10)	(10,10,10)	(10,10,10)
n_3	(6,9,10)	(7,8,10)	(6,9,10)
n_8	(7,8,8)	(7,8,8)	(7,8,8)
n_4	(7,8,10)	(7,8,10)	(7,8,10)
n_5	(6,9,10)	(6,9,10)	(6,9,10)
GL = (6,9,10)		NEXT_MIN = (7,8,8)	

Since GL is still better than NEXT_MIN n_5 is selected and expanded to generate nodes n_6 and n_7.

n	$F(n)$	$F_1(n)$	$F_2(n)$
s	(4,3,4)	(4,3,4)	(10,10,10)
n_1	(6,7,7)	(6,7,7)	(7,8,8)
n_2	(10,10,10)	(10,10,10)	(10,10,10)
n_3	(6,9,10)	(7,8,10)	(6,9,10)
n_8	(7,8,8)	(7,8,8)	(7,8,8)
n_4	(7,8,10)	(7,8,10)	(7,8,10)
n_5	(14,14,14)	(14,14,14)	(14,14,14)
n_6	(14,14,14)	(14,14,14)	(14,14,14)
n_7	(14,14,14)	(14,14,14)	(14,14,14)
GL = (6,9,10)		NEXT_MIN = (7,8,8)	

Now the cost vector of the path, that is (14,14,14), has exceeded not only GL, but also NEXT_MIN. The algorithm therefore backtracks to the node which holds the alternative promised by NEXT_MIN, that is, the algorithm backtracks to node n_1 since $F_2(n_1)$ is equal to NEXT_MIN. The minimum cost vector from the current path, that is (7,8,10), is backed up at $F_1(n_1)$. $\{F_i(n_1)\}$ is sorted in K-order, and n_8 is selected. The value of GL becomes (7,8,8), and NEXT_MIN becomes (7,8,10) which is incidentally the backed up cost vector from n_3.

n	$F(n)$	$F_1(n)$	$F_2(n)$
s	(4,3,4)	(4,3,4)	(10,10,10)
n_1	(7,8,8)	(7,8,10)	(7,8,8)
n_2	(10,10,10)	(10,10,10)	(10,10,10)
n_8	(7,8,8)	(7,8,8)	(7,8,8)
GL = (7,8,8)		NEXT_MIN = (7,8,10)	

Node n_8 is now expanded to generate nodes n_9 and n_{10}.

n	$F(n)$	$F_1(n)$	$F_2(n)$
s	(4,3,4)	(4,3,4)	(10,10,10)
n_1	(7,8,8)	(7,8,10)	(7,8,8)
n_2	(10,10,10)	(10,10,10)	(10,10,10)
n_8	(13,13,13)	(13,13,13)	(13,13,13)
n_9	(13,13,13)	(13,13,13)	(13,13,13)
n_{10}	(13,13,13)	(13,13,13)	(13,13,13)
GL = (7,8,8)		NEXT_MIN = (7,8,10)	

3.5 Memory bounded multiobjective search

Again the path cost vector, that is (13,13,13), has exceeded GL as well as NEXT_MIN. The algorithm backtracks to node n_1, and regenerates n_3 on the basis of the backed up cost vector (7,8,10) which is the current value of NEXT_MIN. The cost vector (13,13,13) is backed up from node n_8. The value of GL becomes (7,8,10), and NEXT_MIN becomes (10,10,10).

n	$F(n)$	$F_1(n)$	$F_2(n)$
s	(4,3,4)	(4,3,4)	(10,10,10)
n_1	(7,8,10)	(7,8,10)	(13,13,13)
n_2	(10,10,10)	(10,10,10)	(10,10,10)
n_3	(7,8,10)	(7,8,10)	(7,8,10)
GL = (7,8,10)	NEXT_MIN = (10,10,10)		

Now, when n_3 is re-expanded, if the cost vectors are evaluated without using *Minf*, then $F(n_4)$ is evaluated as (7,8,10) and $F(n_5)$ is evaluated as (6,9,10) (the same values as those evaluated when they were generated for the first time). On that case node n_5 would have been selected and re-expanded. However, using *Minf*, $F(n_4)$ is evaluated as (7,8,10) and $F(n_5)$ is evaluated as (7,9,10).

n	$F(n)$	$F_1(n)$	$F_2(n)$
s	(4,3,4)	(4,3,4)	(10,10,10)
n_1	(7,8,10)	(7,8,10)	(13,13,13)
n_2	(10,10,10)	(10,10,10)	(10,10,10)
n_3	(7,8,10)	(7,8,10)	(7,9,10)
n_4	(7,8,10)	(7,8,10)	(7,8,10)
n_5	(7,9,10)	(7,9,10)	(7,9,10)
GL = (7,8,10)	NEXT_MIN = (7,9,10)		

Therefore, n_4 is selected and expanded. Subsequently $F(n_{11})$ is evaluated as (7,8,10), and the solution is obtained. It is easy to see that this cost vector dominates all other cost vectors in the explicit search space, and therefore the algorithm terminates without expanding any other node. The unnecessary re-expansion of node n_5 is therefore avoided by virtue of using the function *Minf*. □

Admissibility of MOMA*0

In this section, we prove the admissibility of MOMA*0 and establish the equivalence of MOMA*0 and MOA** in terms of the set of nodes expanded by them. In the following analysis when the terms *greater*, *less*, *minimum*, *maximum* etc. are used with respect to vectors, we mean that the comparison is on the basis of *K-order*.

Lemma # 3.1 *Whenever a node containing the backed-up cost vector of a previously generated (and consequently pruned) path is selected, MOMA*0 will expand at least one new node.*
Proof: MOMA*0 continues the extension of a path P until the representative cost vector of the extended path exceeds the cost vector of the next best alternative. When this happens,

MOMA*0 backtracks up to the node which has this next best promise (now the best). Let this node be t and let u be the child of t in the extended path P'. Since MOMA*0 backs up the F-value while backtracking, $F_i(t) = F(u)$, u being the ith successor of t. The backed up cost vector $F_i(t)$ must have exceeded the previous backed-up vector (otherwise the algorithm will not backtrack). Clearly this backed up cost vector is the representative cost vector of the tip node n of some path generated by extending the path P. When the path P is selected again the node n is guaranteed to be expanded. □

Lemma 3.1 shows that the same path will not be repeatedly re-expanded without any progress. Using this is is now easy to establish the termination of $MOMA^*0$. In order to prove that $MOMA^*0$ is admissible we first show that it expands the same set of nodes as MOA^{**}.

Lemma # 3.2 *$MOMA^*0$ always expands the node n with the minimum F-value $F(n)$. Ties are resolved in favor of nodes at a greater depth.*
Proof: The proof follows from the way NEXT_MIN is maintained and the policy of backtracking to the *deepest* node having a backed-up cost vector equal to NEXT_MIN. □

Lemma # 3.3 *Except for differences due to tie resolutions between nodes having representative cost vectors equal to non-dominated solution cost vectors, the representative cost vectors of new nodes expanded by $MOMA^*0$ occur in the same sequence as the representative cost vectors of nodes expanded by MOA^{**}.*
Proof: MOA^{**} always selects the node having the minimum representative cost vector in the explicit search space. We show that each new node expanded by MOMA*0 is the one having the minimum representative cost vector among all nodes generated up to that point.

When MOMA*0 generates a node n for the first time, $F(n)$ is the same as the representative cost vector from its set of cost vectors. Since $F_i(n)$ denotes the representative cost vector of the tip node of some path through n and its ith successor and $F(n)$ is the minimum among all such $F_i(n)$, it follows that $F(n)$ is actually the minimum among the cost vectors of all leaf nodes in the subtree below node n.

MOMA*0 always selects the node n with the minimum $F(n)$ and extends the path until its cost increases. Clearly $F(n)$ is the minimum representative cost vector among all nodes generated so far. During the course of regeneration there can be no node having a representative cost vector less than $F(n)$ (this is guaranteed by the use of *pathmax* and the function *Minf*). Also no node with a representative cost vector greater than $F(n)$ will be selected until the path having the cost vector $F(n)$ is traced. Thus the first new node that is expanded after selection of node n is the one having the minimum representative cost vector among all nodes generated so far.

Tie resolutions will occur among nodes having this minimum cost vector. If this cost vector is not equal to the cost vector of a non-dominated solution then each of these nodes will be expanded by both algorithms. However, if the cost vector equals that of a non-dominated solution, then depending on the tie resolutions one algorithm may select the solution earlier and prune the other nodes of equal cost. In the worst case situation, the solution node may be selected last. □

3.5 Memory bounded multiobjective search

Lemma 3.3 establishes the equivalence of MOMA*0 and MOA** in terms of the worst case set of nodes expanded by them. The admissibility of MOMA*0 follows from this result.

Theorem # 3.8 *Algorithm MOMA*0 is admissible, that is, it terminates with all non-dominated solutions.*
Proof : The proof follows from lemma 3.1 and lemma 3.3. □

3.5.4 Variants of MOMA*0

The main drawback of MOMA*0 is addressed by the following lemma.

Lemma # 3.4 *If the number of nodes expanded by MOA** is N, then algorithm MOMA*0 expands $O(N^2)$ nodes in the worst case.*
Proof: In the worst case after expanding each new node $MOMA^*0$ may have to backtrack right up to the source node and regenerate the entire portion of the search space that it had pruned earlier before expanding the next new node. Under such a situation it is easy to see that $MOMA^*0$ will expand $O(N^2)$ nodes. □

Lemma 3.4 reflects a standard drawback of many recursive search strategies. Similar results have been obtained for algorithms such as IDA^* [48], prompting researchers to develop techniques such as IDA*_CR [83] and DFS* [79] to reduce the number of node re-expansions in recursive search strategies. In this section we shall suggest extensions of similar techniques to improve the performance of $MOMA^*0$. We also discuss a scheme (in the following sub-section) that is applicable only to the multiobjective framework.

MOMA*0 with multiple back-up cost vectors

When the algorithm MOMA*0 backtracks, it backs up only the minimum cost vector (in K-order) from the pruned space. In case come solution is found during the course of search that dominates the backed up cost vector then the vector becomes useless. Since no other backed up cost vector is available, in the worst case the algorithm may have to explore the same portion of the search space again. The policy of backing up multiple non-dominated cost vectors has the following advantage:

- If all cost vectors are backed up and all of them are subsequently found to be dominated by one or more solutions, then it is possible to prune the portion of the search space below that node forever and save a lot of possible node re-expansions. Also if more than one cost vector is backed up, then whenever the representative cost vector becomes dominated the node may be represented by the next minimum backed up cost vector.

Backing up multiple non-dominated cost vectors also has the following disadvantages.

- Since algorithm $MOMA^*0$ proceeds K-ordered best-first, at each node it needs to compute only the minimum non-dominated cost vector. Computing multiple cost vectors may be expensive for certain heuristic functions.

- The space constraints may prohibit the backing up of multiple cost vectors.

Therefore depending on the situation, there is a scope for trade-off between the number of costs to be backed up and the advantage gained due to reduction in the number of nodes expanded. We shall present experimental results that illustrate such a trade-off on a multiobjective scheduling problem in chapter 4.

MOMA*0 with controlled re-expansions

In this section we suggest the extension of an established technique from the conventional search model for controlling node re-expansions in backtracking heuristic search strategies. In the conventional model the following result has been established [48] for strategies such as IDA^*:

- If for some constant b (such that $b^K = N$ for some integer K), b^i new nodes are expanded in the ith iteration, then the worst case complexity of the strategy reduces from $O(N^2)$ to $O(N)$.

Based on this result, the algorithm IDA^*_CR was developed by Sarkar *et al* [83]. In each iteration i, IDA^*_CR performs a depth-first branch and bound with a cutoff value x, which is set in way so as to ensure that at least b^i new nodes are expanded. To determine the cutoff value for the next iteration, IDA^*_CR uses a bucketing technique for grouping the node costs that exceed the cut-off of the current iteration.

A similar technique may be used to reduce the number of node re-expansions in MOMA*0. We may define an iteration to be the set of operations between successive assignments of new values to GL. An iteration ends when there are no more paths with cost less than or equal to the current value of GL (in K-order). By using a suitable bucketing technique it is possible to group the representative cost vectors of nodes which exceeded GL in an iteration. The extended algorithm then simply assigns GL a new vector such that in the ith iteration GL exceeds (or equals) the representative cost vectors of at least b^i new nodes. After a new vector is assigned to GL, this algorithm searches the space below the tip node of the current path with the new GL as cut-off. The remaining operations are identical to that of MOMA*0.

The algorithm MOMA*

One way of controlling excessive node regeneration is to prune nodes only when the given memory is exhausted. In the conventional search model the algorithm MA^* [10] uses such an idea. The algorithm $MOMA^*$ is an extension of MA^* to the multiobjective framework with suitable modifications. The algorithm makes use of *K-order* to prune away the nodes having the maximum representative cost vector in K-order. The operation of the algorithm is similar to that of MOMA*0 except that the pruning and cost back-up mechanism is initiated only when the given memory (which is specified through a parameter called MAX) is exhausted. The outline of this algorithm is given in appendix A.1.

The admissibility of MOMA* follows from the admissibility of MOMA*0. In addition, the algorithm has the following property. We state it here without a proof.

- The algorithm MOMA* never uses more memory than $MAX+ \mid C^* \mid$, where MAX is the given parameter depicting the additional amount of memory available and $\mid C^* \mid$ is the number of nodes in the longest non-dominated path in the search space.

3.6 Searching with inadmissible heuristics

The admissibility and optimality properties of best-first search algorithms such as A* and MOA* are subject to the admissibility of the heuristic function. Though an inadmissible heuristic function may not be able to guarantee admissibility, search algorithms using such heuristics are sometimes found to converge to the solution much faster than weaker admissible heuristics. The problem of searching with inadmissible heuristics has been well studied within the conventional search model [1, 25, 75]. This section presents preliminary results obtained by us on multiobjective search with inadmissible heuristics.

In order to avoid exhaustive search of the state-space, the following basic policies are adopted by strategies such as MOA^* and MOA^{**}.

- The node which is selected from OPEN for expansion must be non-dominated in OPEN.

- If every cost vector of a node is dominated by the cost vectors of already obtained solutions, then the node will never be selected for expansion.

If the above policies are not adopted then it may be easily shown that the search turns out to be exhaustive in many situations. We now show that if the heuristic function is inadmissible, then admissibility of the algorithm cannot be guaranteed without relaxing the above policies.

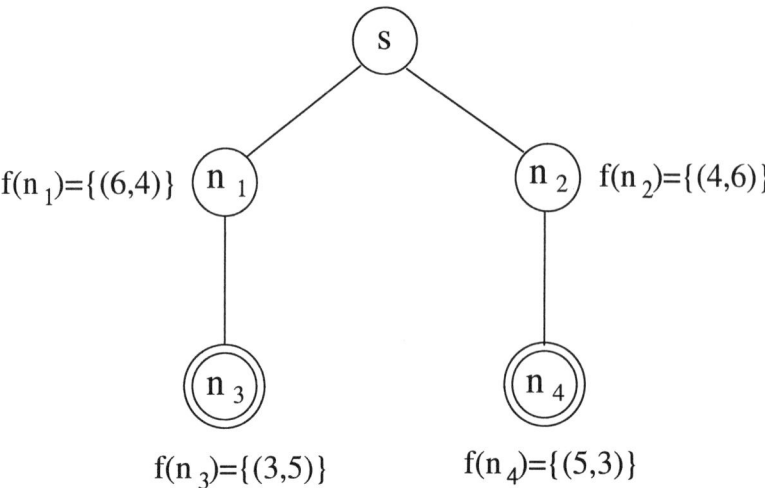

Figure 3.5: Multiobjective graph with inadmissible heuristics

Theorem # 3.9 *If the heuristic function is inadmissible then no algorithm is guaranteed to find all non-dominated solutions unless it expands dominated nodes also.*
Proof: We prove the result by constructing a problem instance where the expansion of a dominated node becomes mandatory. Let us consider the graph in Fig 3.5. At first node s is expanded to generate node n_1 having the single cost vector (6,4) and node n_2 having the single cost vector (4,6). Since $F(n_1)$ and $F(n_2)$ are mutually non-dominated either of them may be selected first by the search strategy. Let us consider both the cases.

1. If n_1 is selected, then the goal node n_3 of cost vector (3,5) is generated. Since $F(n_3)$ dominates $F(n_2)$, n_3 is selected next and the solution of cost vector (3,5) is recorded. This cost vector dominates $F(n_2)$. Therefore any strategy that adopts the policy of not expanding dominated nodes will not expand n_2 and so will never find the other non-dominated goal node n_4 of cost (5,3).

2. If n_2 is selected prior to n_1, then by a similar reasoning the non-dominated solution n_3 will never be found unless the dominated node n_1 is expanded.

Thus, unless the search strategy expands a dominated node, it will not be able to find all non-dominated solutions. □

The above result also shows that depending upon the policy adopted by an algorithm to decide which nodes to expand first, different sets of solution nodes will be discovered by the search. In this section we analyze the conditions for a given solution path to be discovered by MOA**. In the following discussion when the terms *greater, less, minimum, maximum* etc. are used with respect to vectors, we mean that the comparison is on the basis of *K-order*.

3.6 Searching with inadmissible heuristics

Def # 3.7 [pmax]:
We define a function called "pmax" as follows. Given a path P, $pmax[P]$ returns the maximum of the representative cost vectors of all nodes on the path P. We shall also refer to the vector returned by $pmax[P]$ as "pmax of P". □

Def # 3.8 [pmax-ordering]:
We define a strict ordering on the search paths as follows. We shall refer to this ordering as "pmax-ordering".

Given any two paths P_1 and P_2:
1. If $\text{pmax}[P_1] < \text{pmax}[P_2]$ then $P_1 < P_2$ based on pmax-ordering.
2. If $\text{pmax}[P_2] < \text{pmax}[P_1]$ then $P_2 < P_1$ based on pmax-ordering.
3. If $\text{pmax}[P_1] = \text{pmax}[P_2]$ then
    3.1 Let $n_1 \in P_1$ and $n_2 \in P_2$ be the shallowest nodes in P_1 and P_2 respectively such that the representative cost vector of n_1 equals $pmax[P_1]$ and the representative cost vector of n_2 equals $pmax[P_2]$.
    3.2 If n_1 and n_2 are the same node then
        If the node is a tip node then
            $P_1 < P_2$ or $P_2 < P_1$ (arbitrarily, based on the tie-breaking rules).
        else
        3.2.1 Let P_1' be the subpath of P_1 from n_1 onwards
            and P_2' be the subpath of P_2 from n_2 onwards
        3.2.2 If $P_1' < P_2'$ on pmax-ordering
            then $P_1 < P_2$ on pmax-ordering.
        3.2.3 If $P_2' < P_1'$ on pmax-ordering
            then $P_2 < P_1$ on pmax-ordering.
        else when n_1 and n_2 are different nodes then
            $P_1 < P_2$ or $P_2 < P_1$ (arbitrarily, based on the tie-breaking rules). □

Def # 3.9 Eligible node:
We say that a node n is "eligible" for expansion if it satisfies at least one of the following conditions.

1. Let P_{min} be the minimum solution path based on "pmax-ordering". If n belongs to P_{min} then n is eligible.

2. A node n is eligible for expansion if it has at least one cost vector $f(n)$ which is non-dominated by the cost vector of every eligible solution path P such that $pmax[P]$ is less than $f(n)$. A path is eligible if all its nodes are eligible.

□

Based on the above definitions, the following properties are easy to establish for the algorithm MOA**.

- The necessary and sufficient condition for a node n to be expanded is that all nodes on the path $P(s, n)$ from the start node s to the node n are *eligible*.

- If two paths P_1 and P_2 are eligible, then P_1 is generated prior to P_2 if and only if $P_1 < P_2$ in *pmax-ordering*.

- MOA^{**} finds the solution paths in the *pmax-ordered* sequence of the paths.

If we also relax the assumption that any cost vector of a finite path dominates every cost vector of an infinite path (assumption 3.3), then infinite paths may have finite cost vectors. If such a path is *eligible* up to infinite depth, then it is easy to see that MOA** will not terminate. Taking all these aspects into account, the general conditions of admissibility of MOA^{**} may be stated as follows.

Admissibility conditions of MOA**
MOA^{**} terminates with all non-dominated solutions iff:
1. There is no infinite path which is eligible up to infinite depth, and
2. Every non-dominated solution path is eligible, and
3. The pmax-ordering of the solution paths describe the same sequence as the representative cost vector of the paths based on K-ordering.

The third condition may be relaxed by modifying step 5 of MOA** as follows:

5. [IDENTIFY SOLUTIONS]
If n is a goal node then
5.1 Put n in SOLUTION_GOALS and its cost in SOLUTION_COSTS.
5.2 Remove dominated solutions (if any) from SOLUTION_COSTS.
5.3 GoTo [Step 2].

The introduction of step 5.2 becomes necessary because if the third condition is relaxed then the solution nodes may not arrive in the K-ordered sequence of their cost vectors and it is possible that some solution node entered in SOLUTION_GOALS is dominated by the cost vector of some solution found later.

3.7 Extension to graphs

In this section we extend the algorithm MOA^{**} to graphs. The algorithm $MOMA^*0$ requires no modification and may be applied to graph search in its present form.

While searching graphs MOA^{**} maintains a list G(n) at each node n which contains the non-dominated cost vectors of paths from the source node s to the node n. For each vector $g(n)$ in $G(n)$, a pointer to the parent on the corresponding path is also maintained. For extending MOA** to graphs, only Step 6 needs to be modified as follows (we assume that the list CLOSED is initialized to ϕ in Step 1).

3.8 Conclusion

6. [EXPAND]
    6.1 Generate all successors of n
    6.2 For each successor m of n
        6.2.1 Calculate $\hat{G}(m)$ as follows:
            6.2.1.1 For each $g(n) \in G(n)$
                Put $g(m) \leftarrow g(n) + c(n, m)$ in $\hat{G}(m)$
        6.2.2 If $m \in CLOSED$ then
            6.2.2.1 Remove each g(m) from $\hat{G}(m)$ such that
                g(m) is dominated by some $g'(m) \in G(m)$
            6.2.2.2 If $\hat{G}(m) = \phi$ then
                Goto [Step 6.2]
                Else Add $\hat{G}(m)$ to G(m) and put m in OPEN
            6.2.2.3 Goto [Step 6.2.5]
        6.2.3 If $m \in OPEN$ then
            6.2.3.1 Remove each g(m) from $\hat{G}(m)$ such that
                g(m) is dominated by some $g'(m) \in G(m)$
            6.2.3.2 Add $\hat{G}(m)$ to G(m)
        6.2.4 If $m \notin OPEN$ and $m \notin CLOSED$ then
            6.2.4.1 Rename $\hat{G}(m)$ to G(m)
            6.2.4.2 Put m in OPEN
        6.2.5 Calculate $\hat{H}(m)$ of heuristic vectors using *pathmax* on P(n,m)
        6.2.6 Add $\hat{H}(m)$ to $H(m)$ and remove dominated heuristics from $H(m)$
        6.2.7 Compute the set set $F(m)$ by adding the cost vectors in $H(m)$ with $G(m)$.
        6.2.8 Determine the minimum cost vector in $F(m)$ using K-ordering.
            Declare that cost as the representative cost vector of m.
        6.2.9 Enter m in OPEN.

In multiobjective search of graphs, a node is brought from CLOSED to OPEN if it is generated along some other path whose cost vector is non-dominated by the other cost vectors in G(n).

3.8 Conclusion

In this chapter we have addressed two major topics under multiobjective state space search. The first has been to refine the basic search scheme proposed by Stewart and White [91] by incorporating algorithmic improvements. We have extended the standard technique of *pathmax* to the multiobjective framework and have shown that in a way it is more significant in the multiobjective model than in the conventional model. We have also incorporated ideas such as using an induced total order (such as K-order) on the partial order search.

The other major issue addressed in this chapter has been to develop memory bounded search strategies. We have shown that the major difficulty in extending standard memory bounded search schemes to this model is due to the presence of multiple candidate back-up cost vectors in the pruned space, and that the problem can be resolved by using a total order on the search. We have presented the algorithm MOMA*0 to establish this fact.

In chapter 4 we shall use the techniques developed in this chapter to solve three practical multiobjective search problems. We shall also compare the performance of the strategies presented (and suggested) in this chapter with straight-forward generalizations of single objective search strategies to study the effectiveness of the multiobjective search techniques.

Chapter 4

Applications of Multiobjective Search

This chapter addresses applications of multiobjective search. The approach is two-fold. The first is to demonstrate the modeling and solving of practical multi-criteria optimization problems using the multiobjective search scheme. The other is to compare the relative efficiency of the multiobjective search techniques developed in chapter 3 (such as MOA^{**} and $MOMA^*0$) with straight-forward generalizations of standard single objective search strategies (such as A^* and *Depth-first Branch and Bound*).

We model the following three problems in the multiobjective framework and apply the search techniques developed in chapter 3 to solve them:

1. **The Operator Scheduling Problem:** The problem is a special case of the general resource scheduling problem [14]. It is one of the major problems in VLSI high level synthesis [65].

2. **The Channel Routing Problem:** This problem is an integral part of VLSI circuit design, particularly in the layout synthesis phase[26].

3. **The Log Cutting Problem:** This is a variant of the bin packing problem also known as the roll cutting problem [29].

In this chapter we also present experimental results that demonstrate the trade-off between the number of cost vectors backed up by a multiobjective memory bounded search strategy and the total number of nodes expanded by it.

The chapter is organized as follows. In the sections 4.1, 4.2 and 4.3 we describe the modeling of the problems. Section 4.4 presents the experimental results and performance comparisons.

4.1 The Operator Scheduling Problem

The goal of high level synthesis is to produce Register Transfer Level (RTL) designs from a behavioral description of the circuit [65]. An RTL data path consists of functional modules and registers which are interconnected via multiplexers, buses and wires. Starting from the description of the circuit behavior in a hardware description language, a number of tasks are involved in synthesis. These include scheduling of operations, allocation of resources and binding of resources to abstract entities.

The main difficulty which the designer encounters while synthesizing RTL datapaths is selecting the design which best meets the goals while satisfying the constraints. The designer trades off the amount of parallelism and the amount of resource sharing to arrive at a satisfactory design. RTL designs lie in a *design space* [43], which can be modeled as a two-dimensional plane with area and delay as its two axes. A *design point* represents a design in this space. In such a two-dimensional design space, the cheapest (least area) and the fastest designs delimit the design space boundary. Not all designs are of equal quality. A design implementation is inferior when there exists at least one other implementation which performs better in one or more figures of merit, all other figures of merit being at least equal. For example, a design D_1 using t_1 time steps and a_1 area *dominates* a design D_2 using t_2 time steps and a_2 area if:

$$t_1 < t_2 \text{ and } a_1 \leq a_2 \qquad OR \qquad t_1 \leq t_2 \text{ and } a_1 < a_2$$

A design D_i is *non-dominated* in a set of designs if there does not exist any design in that set which dominates D_i.

Different scheduling algorithms presented in the past may be classified into two broad categories:

1. Strategies such as the one used in MAHA [72] and FDS [73] used in HAL [74], which attempt to minimize overall operator cost (area) assuming that the number of time steps is pre-specified.

2. Strategies such as the one used in the BUD system [64], which attempt to maximize speed by minimizing the number of time steps assuming that the number of different operators are given.

Some synthesis systems, such as ADAM [44] accepts an absolute value of either area or performance as a design constraint and optimizes the other. Since it may not be possible to specify accurate design constraints a priori, the system provides for progressive refinement of constraints. The complexity of this approach has motivated researchers to develop predictors to determine appropriate design constraints prior to design space exploration [43].

In this section, we describe the multiobjective scheme for solving this problem. From the multiobjective viewpoint the problem may be formally defined as follows.

4.1 The Operator Scheduling Problem

Def # 4.1 The Operator Scheduling Problem:

Input: An acyclic data flow graph $G(O, E)$, where

$O \equiv \{\theta_1, \theta_2, \ldots, \theta_N\}$ is the set of vertices representing the set of operations to be scheduled.

$E \equiv \{e_1, e_2, \ldots, e_M\}$ is the set of directed edges in the DFG which model precedence relationships among operations. An edge $e_i = (\theta_p, \theta_q)$ implies that the operation θ_p must be scheduled before the operation θ_q. The *area* C^a of each operator type a and the number of time steps required by it are also inputs to the problem.

Objective: To determine the set of non-dominated $<area, delay>$ schedules for the given data flow graph.

The following example illustrates the multiobjective approach to this problem.

Example # 4.1 For the data flow graph shown in Fig 4.1, there are three non-dominated schedules. The schedule requiring the minimum number of time steps (i.e. 4 time steps) uses 4 operators. The second schedule requires one more time step, but only 3 operators. The third schedule requires 8 time steps and only 2 operators. Since there are two types of operators, a schedule with fewer operators is not possible. It should be noted that other schedules are possible which require the same number of time steps and the same number of operators as one of the schedules in Fig 4.1. We treat such schedules to be equivalent. The objective of multiobjective search is to obtain a set of non-dominated solutions such that the cost vector of each solution is distinct. □

4.1.1 Notation & Terminology

The following notation has been used to describe the operator scheduling problem.

s:	The *start node* representing the scheduling problem instance.
n,m:	Other nodes representing partially solved problems (subproblems) of the original problem.
h_m:	A heuristic vector (t, c_θ), where c_θ represents the estimated total operator area required to complete the scheduling of the subproblem represented by node m in a total of t time steps.
H_m:	The set of 2-dimensional heuristic vectors of node m.
f_m:	The representative cost vector of node m.
DFG:	The given acyclic data flow graph for the scheduling problem.
T_c:	The size of the longest (*critical*) path in the DFG.
C^a:	Area of the operator type a.
θ_i, θ_j:	Operations.
$ASAP$:	The *as soon as possible* schedule.
$asap_i$:	The ASAP time step of operation θ_i.
$ALAP^t$:	The *as late as possible* schedule given t number of time steps.
$alap_i^t$:	The ALAP time step of operation θ_i given t number of time steps.

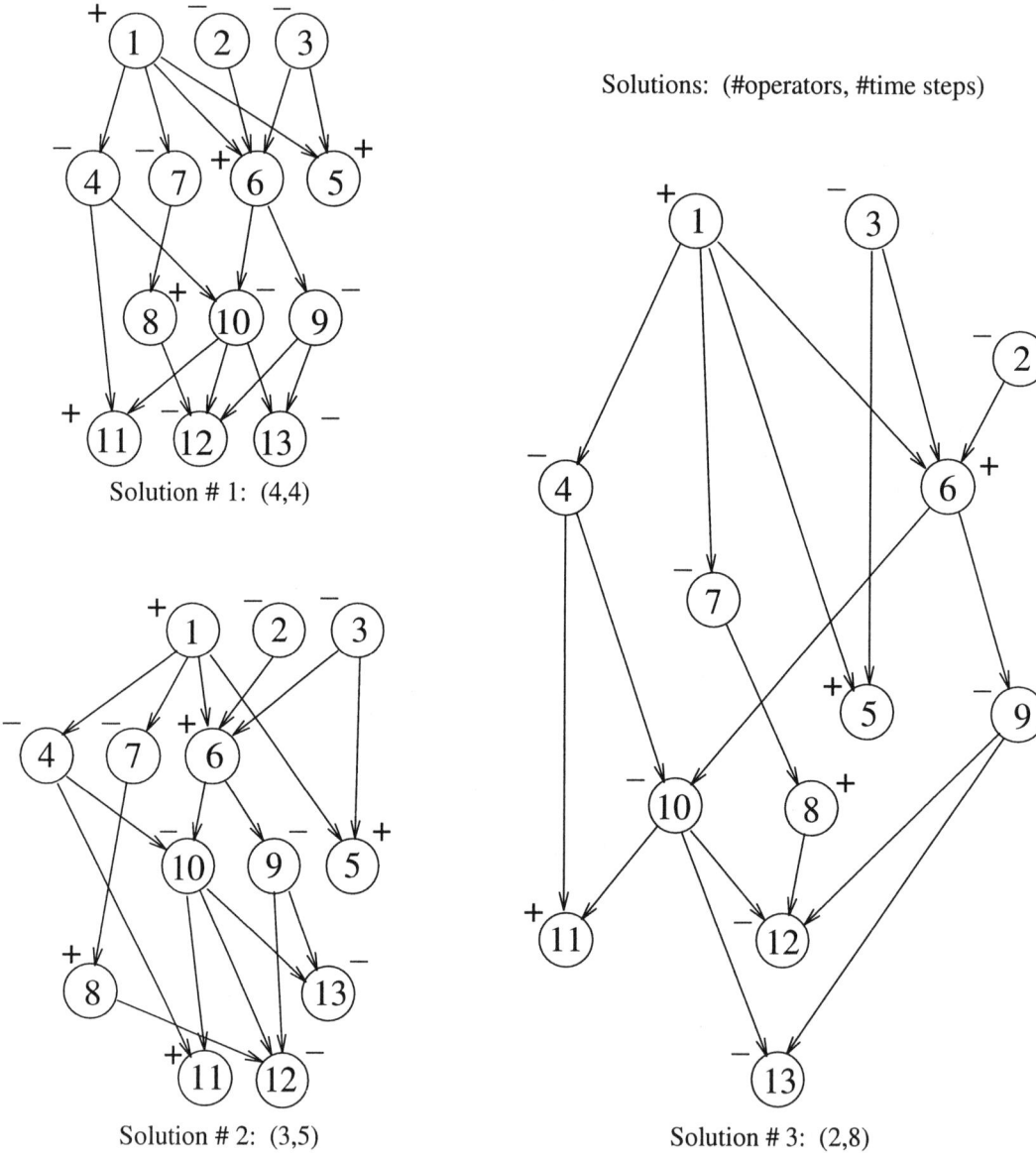

Figure 4.1: A Set of Non-dominated Schedules

4.1 The Operator Scheduling Problem

The definitions of *dominance* and *K-ordering* follows from the chapters 2 and 3 respectively. Since only two objectives are involved we refer to K-ordering as *2-ordering*.

4.1.2 Algorithm MObj_Schedule

In this section we extend the algorithm MOA^{**} presented in chapter 3 to develop a multiobjective search based scheduling algorithm. The following assumptions are made about the problem:

- All operations are single time step operations.
- Chaining of operations in a time step is not permitted.
- Area of registers is not considered.

The objective of making these assumptions is to convey the basic issues in simple terms. The proposed algorithm can be extended to take into account more general cases as well.

Some edges in the DFG may be redundant because the precedence relationship denoted by them may automatically follow from other edges. For example, an edge $e_i = (\theta_p, \theta_q)$ is redundant if there exists a directed path consisting of two or more edges from θ_p to θ_q. In the first step of the proposed algorithm, all such transitive edges are removed from the DFG.

The state space is a tree that may be described as follows. The start node represents the original problem where none of the operations have been scheduled. Every other non-terminal node in the search space represents a partially solved subproblem of the original problem where some of the operations have been scheduled and the others are yet to be scheduled. The child node of a given node is a subproblem having one more scheduled operation than its parent. The solution nodes are those where all the operations have been scheduled.

It is implicitly assumed that the heuristic function is admissible. Thus each heuristic vector at a node in the search space either dominates or is equal to the cost vector of one or more non-dominated solution in the subtree below it. The scheme for node selection and expansion is as follows:

- In each iteration, the node n having the minimum representative cost vector in 2-order is selected from OPEN.

- The operation θ_i with the minimum ASAP time step is selected from all operations which remain to be scheduled in the subproblem represented by the node n.

- Distinct child nodes are generated by scheduling the selected operation θ_i in the different time steps where it can be scheduled. Given t time steps to schedule all the operations, it is easy to see that the operation θ_i can be scheduled in every time step from $asap_i$ to $alap_i^t$. Since the maximum number of time steps can be at

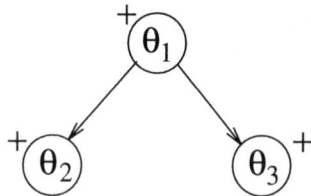

Figure 4.2: A Data Flow Graph

most equal to the number of operations T, the operation θ_i can be scheduled in all time steps from $asap_i$ to $alap_i^T$.

- Each child obtained by scheduling the operation θ_i in a distinct time step represents a distinct subproblem of scheduling the remaining operations.

We illustrate this process through the following example.

Example # 4.2 Consider the simple data flow graph in Fig 4.2. To schedule all the operations, a minimum of two time steps and a maximum of three time steps are required. The ASAP time step of operation θ_1 is t_1, and that of the other two operations is t_2. Initially OPEN consists of the source node s which represents the given problem. In the first iteration the node s is selected and the operation having the minimum ASAP time step (that is, θ_1) is scheduled at t_1. Clearly θ_1 cannot be scheduled at any other time step, hence s has a single child node n_1 which represents the subproblem of scheduling θ_2 and θ_3 given that θ_1 is fixed at t_1.

In the next iteration node n_1 is selected from OPEN. Since θ_2 and θ_3 have the same ASAP time step, either of them may be selected. Without loss of generality let us assume that θ_2 is selected first. Since θ_2 can be scheduled in either t_2 or t_3, node n_1 will have two children, namely n_2 which represents the subproblem of scheduling θ_3 given that θ_1 and θ_2 are scheduled in t_1 and t_2 respectively, and n_3 which represents the subproblem of scheduling θ_3 given that θ_1 and θ_2 are scheduled in t_1 and t_3 respectively. Nodes n_2 and n_3 are now entered in OPEN. When n_2 is selected, again two children are generated (both of which are solution nodes) since θ_3 can be scheduled either in t_2 or in t_3. When node n_3 is selected, θ_3 must be scheduled in t_2 (which would be wasted otherwise), and therefore only one child of n_3 will be generated (which is also a solution node). □

Example 4.2 only shows the branching of the state space and the process of node expansion. The algorithm presented in the next sub-section makes use of the heuristic vectors evaluated at each node as well as the partial order imposed by dominance to effect reasonable amount of pruning so that the search scheme is feasible.

The outline of MObj_Schedule

The algorithm *MObj_Schedule* is an adaptation of the algorithm MOA** presented in chapter 3 on the state space of the multiobjective scheduling problem. The outline of

4.1 The Operator Scheduling Problem

the algorithm is as follows.

Algorithm MObj_Schedule

1. **[INITIALIZE]**
    1.1 Remove the transitive edges in the DFG.
    1.2 Find the *as soon as possible* (ASAP) schedule of the DFG.
        1.2.1 Let $asap_i$ denote the ASAP time step of operation θ_i
        1.2.2 Assign a distinct number b_i to each operation θ_i
            such that $b_i < b_j$ if $asap_i < asap_j$
    1.3 OPEN $\leftarrow s$; SOLUTION_COSTS $\leftarrow \phi$;
    1.4 Compute the representative cost vector f_s of node s

2. **[TERMINATE]**
    If OPEN is empty then Terminate.

3. **[SELECT]**
    Remove the node n with the minimum representative cost vector from OPEN
    Resolve ties in favor of goal nodes, else arbitrarily.

4. **[DOMINANCE CHECKING]**
    If f_n is dominated by some cost vector in SOLUTION_COSTS then
    4.1 Remove dominated heuristic vectors from H_n.
    4.2 If H_n is empty, then remove node n from the memory, otherwise find the
        new representative cost vector f_n and enter n in OPEN.
    4.3 Goto [Step 2]

5. **[IDENTIFY SOLUTION]**
    If every operation at n have been scheduled, then
    5.1 Enter f_n in SOLUTION_COSTS and output the solution.
    5.2 Goto [Step 2].

6. **[EXPAND]**
    6.1 Let θ_i be the operation with minimum number b_i, such that θ_i is
        not yet scheduled in the sub-problem represented by the node n.
    6.2 Let $alap_i^T$ be the latest time step in which the operation θ_i can be
        scheduled if only one operation is allowed in a time step.
    6.3 For all time steps k between $asap_i$ and $alap_i^T$
        6.3.1 Generate a child m of node n in which all operations θ_j such that $b_j < b_i$
            are scheduled exactly as in the partial solution represented by
            node n, and θ_i is scheduled in the kth time step.
        6.3.2 Compute the representative cost vector f_m of node m.
        6.3.3 Insert node m in OPEN.

7. **[ITERATE]**
    Goto [Step 2]

The algorithm *MObj_Schedule* can also use given constraints on *time* and *operator area* to prune the search space and find all non-dominated solutions within the given constraints. The constraints may be specified as (*time,area*) vectors. Given a set of constraints, *MObj_Schedule* will expand a node n only if at least one of its cost vectors dominate one or more constraint vectors. The remaining portion of the algorithm remains exactly as above.

Generation of heuristics

The heuristic function used by us in our experiments computes admissible heuristic vectors by following the lower bound generation scheme proposed by Alok Kumar *et al* [57] for this problem. We describe this scheme in brief.

Given t time steps in which the scheduling has to be completed, the ASAP time step and the ALAP time step of an operation θ_i is denoted by $asap_i$ and $alap_i^t$ respectively. It should be noted that while $asap_i$ is independent of the number of time steps t allowed for the schedule, $alap_i^t$ is a function of t. The *degree of freedom* of an operation θ_i when t time steps are allowed for the schedule is defined as follows:

$$DOF^t(\theta_i) = alap_i^t - asap_i$$

The total operator area C_θ is given by:

$$C_\theta = \sum_a C^a . N^a$$

where C^a denotes the given *area* of operator type a and N^a is a lowerbound on the number of operators of type a used for scheduling the DFG in t time steps. N^a is computed by considering all possible ways of scheduling the operations of type a in the DFG so that the total number of time steps required is t. Let $X_{i,j}^a$ represent the number of operations of type a that must be scheduled between time steps i and j. Then N^a is computed as follows:

$$N^a = \max\left\{\left\lceil \frac{X_{i,j}^a}{j-i+1} \right\rceil, \quad i=1\ldots t, \quad j=1\ldots t\right\}$$

Let $Y_{i,z}^a$ represent the number of operations of type a with ASAP i and DOF less than or equal to z. $X_{i,j}^a$ can be computed in terms of $Y_{i,z}^a$ as follows:

$$X_{i,j}^a = \sum_{k=i}^{j} Y_{k,j-k}^a$$

Computation of $Y_{i,z}^a$ is trivial once the ASAP schedule and the DOF of each operation is computed.

Given the value of t, it is possible to compute a lowerbound on the operator area using the above method. In order to estimate the operator area when some operations are

4.2 The Channel Routing Problem

already scheduled, the *asap* and *alap* values of all scheduled operations are fixed to the respective time steps where they have been scheduled, and then the same computation is used.

4.2 The Channel Routing Problem

Channel routing is one of the major tasks in VLSI layouts synthesis [9, 26, 38]. There are several models for this problem. The most common of these is called the *two layer non-overlap Manhattan model*. The multiobjective search based channel router presented in this section is based on this model.

The input to a channel routing problem is a pair of *netlists*. A *netlist* is a row of terminals. Each terminal is marked by a non-negative integer that indicates the *net* to which that terminal belongs. Dummy terminals (which do not belong to any *net*) are marked by zero. The two rows of terminals corresponding to the two netlists are placed horizontally and parallel to each other with some amount to space (called the *channel*) between them. The channel routing task is to connect the terminals belonging to the same *net* by laying connecting wires on the *channel*.

Fig 4.3 shows several solutions for the following problem instance in the two layer Manhattan model.

Top row: 1 2 0 3 0 4 0 5 0 6 0 6 7 7 0
Bottom row: 0 1 0 2 0 3 0 4 0 5 6 7 0 8 8

The basic elements of the two layer Manhattan model are as follows:

- In this model only horizontal and vertical wire segments are allowed. In terms of fabrication the implication is that the horizontal wire segments and the vertical wire segments are laid on two different layers. A horizontal wire segment can be connected to a vertical wire segment by a holed-through connection called a *via*.

- It is assumed that the channel is an an implicit rectilinear grid consisting of horizontal *tracks* and vertical *columns*. The horizontal wires are laid on the *tracks* and the vertical wires are laid on the *columns*. The terminals are positioned on the intersecting points of the columns with the top and bottom tracks.

- If two horizontal wire segments are connected by a vertical wire segment, then the connection is called a *dogleg*. In Fig 4.3 the first, second and third solutions use five, two and one *doglegs*, respectively, while the fourth solution does not use any *dogleg*.

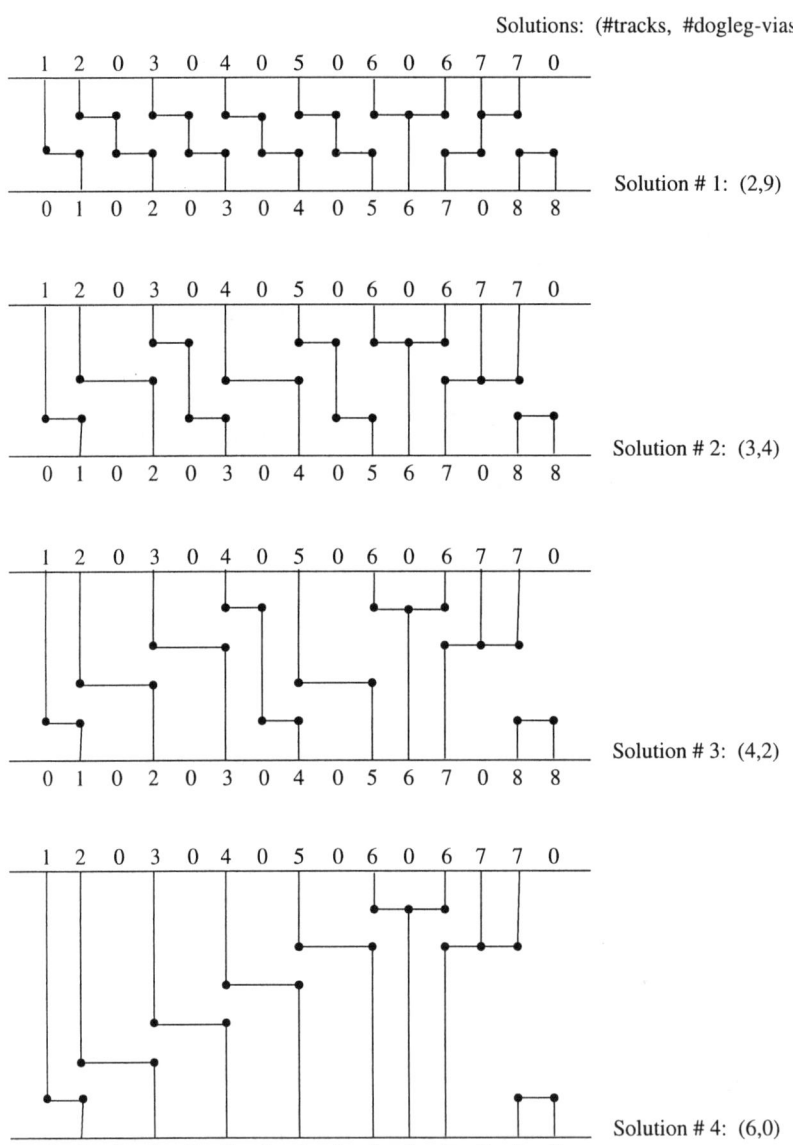

Figure 4.3: A Set of Non-dominated Layouts

4.2 The Channel Routing Problem

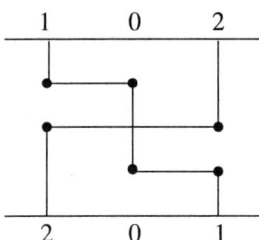

Figure 4.4: Channel illustrating cyclic vertical constraints

In some problem instances the use of *doglegs* is mandatory in order to complete the routing. For example, the following problem instance cannot be solved in the two layer Manhattan model without using a *dogleg*.

Top row: 1 0 2
Bottom row: 2 0 1

Fig 4.4 shows a layout for this problem using one *dogleg*. One popular way of detecting such instances is to construct a directed *vertical constraint graph*, such that each net N_i is represented by a vertex v_i in the graph, and there exists an edge from v_i to v_j iff there is a column k such that net N_i has a terminal on the top of column k and net N_j has a terminal on the bottom of column k. If the vertical constraint graph contains cycles then the use of *doglegs* is mandatory.

The objective of a channel router is to complete the routing using minimum number of tracks and vias. The number of tracks reflect the *area* required for routing. Each via increases the capacitance of the net and contributes to the delay through the net. Reducing the number of vias is also important for other reasons such as increasing the yield and reliability of the chip.

In the two layer non-overlap Manhattan model, there are several well known channel routers [26, 80, 93, 9] that attempt to route the nets using a minimum number of tracks. Since minimizing the number of tracks is the primary concern of these algorithms, most of them tend to use a large number of doglegs to resolve the vertical constraints and complete the routing using minimum number of tracks. Though introduction of doglegs decreases the channel width significantly, each dogleg adds one or two additional vias in the net thereby increasing the delay through the net.

In recent times, many new models have been proposed for the channel routing problem. Most of these models have emerged by relaxing the constraints on the two-layer Manhattan model. Some of the interesting models are as follows:

- The *multilayer channel routing* model [77, 6, 59] allows more than two layers for routing.

- In *topological routing* model [60, 85] the router attempts to minimize the number of vias by relaxing the constraints imposed by the grid-like layout in the Manhattan model.

- The *over-the-cell routing* model [16, 40, 39] utilizes the region above the cells to route some of the wires.

The objective of our work has been to address the problem in the basic two-layer model using multiobjective search based techniques. The *number of tracks* and the *number of vias due to doglegs* represent the dual dimensions of the problem. The multiobjective viewpoint to this problem is shown in Fig 4.3 where the four non-dominated solutions illustrate the trade-off between the number of tracks and the number of additional vias introduced as a result of doglegs.

4.2.1 Notation & Terminology

The following notation has been used in this section.

s:	The *start node* representing the Channel Routing problem instance.
n,m:	Other nodes representing partially solved problems (subproblems) of the original problem.
g_m:	The accrued cost vector $<t,v>$, where t represents the number of tracks completed and v represents the number of vias used in the subproblem represented by node m.
h_m:	A heuristic vector $<t,v>$, where t and v represent the estimated number of tracks and vias required to complete the subproblem at node m.
f_m:	The representative cost vector of node m.
N_i:	Net i. Nonterminals are represented by zero.
d_k:	Density of column k, that is, the number of nets intersecting k.
d_{max}:	Channel density. It is the maximum of d_k, $\forall k$.
$T(i)$:	i^{th} terminal on the top of a channel.
$B(i)$:	i^{th} terminal on the bottom of a channel.

The definitions of *dominance* and *K-ordering* follows from the chapters 2 and 3 respectively. Since only two objectives are involved we refer to K-ordering as *2-ordering*.

4.2.2 Algorithm MObj_Route

The number of possible solutions of a typical instance of the channel routing problem can be prohibitively large, hence it is clearly infeasible to explore the entire solution space. Considering the search effort involved we chose to adopt the policy of searching the more promising portions of the search space defined by certain constraints on the layout of the wires and some precedences among the nets.

The search space is an implicit tree defined as follows. The start node represents the given problem. Every other non-terminal node in the search space represents a partially

4.2 The Channel Routing Problem

solved subproblem of the original problem. The routing mechanism proceeds on a track by track basis starting from the topmost track, so that a node at depth k represents a subproblem where wire segments have been laid out on the top $k-1$ tracks. The solution nodes are those where no more wire segment remains to be laid.

It is assumed that the heuristic function is admissible. The scheme for node expansion is as follows:

- Each child of a node is generated by assigning a distinct combination of wire segments to the topmost empty track of the subproblem represented by the node. Thus each child represents a distinct subproblem of laying out the remaining wire segments using additional tracks.

- The combination of wire segments to be laid out on a track can be selected in many different ways. Clearly it is infeasible to consider all possible combinations. In our experiments we have used two greedy approaches to determine two different combinations so that the branching factor of the search tree is restricted to two. These greedy approaches make use of judiciously defined constraints so that the search is restricted to a relatively small portion of the entire search space.

The approach presented in this section may also be considered as a general framework for combining greedy algorithms. This is particularly useful from the multiobjective point of view since the combination of wire segments chosen by some greedy algorithms may increase the number of doglegs by breaking too many nets while others may impose restrictions on using doglegs and end up using many extra tracks.

The outline of MObj_Route

The algorithm *MObj_Route* is an extension of the algorithm MOA** presented in chapter 3 on the state space of the channel routing problem. The outline of the algorithm is presented below.

Since the solutions are obtained in an increasing 2-ordered sequence of their cost vectors, successive solutions use more number of tracks than the previous ones. It follows that the successive non-dominated solutions must have less number of vias than the previous solutions. Hence, the number of vias used by the most recent solution can be used as an upperbound on the number of vias for all remaining nodes. The number of vias used by the most recent solution is stored in a scalar variable MIN_VIA.

Algorithm MObj_Route

1. **[INITIALIZE]**
   OPEN $\leftarrow$ s ; SOLUTION_COSTS $\leftarrow \phi$;
   Compute f_s. Set MIN_VIA $\leftarrow \infty$

2. **[TERMINATE]**
   If OPEN is empty then Terminate.

3. **[SELECT]**
   Remove the node n in OPEN with the minimum cost vector based on 2-ordering.
   Resolve ties in favor of goal nodes, else arbitrarily.

4. **[DOMINANCE CHECK]**
   If the number of vias in f_n is greater than or equal to MIN_VIA then
       4.1 Remove node n from the memory.
       4.2 Goto [Step 2].

5. **[IDENTIFY SOLUTIONS]**
   If n is a goal node then
       5.1 Enter f_n in SOLUTION_COSTS and output the solution.
       5.2 Set MIN_VIA to the number of vias in f_n.
       5.3 Goto [Step 2].

6. **[EXPAND]**
   Generate the successors of node n by laying out various combinations of
   wire segments on the topmost track of the problem represented by node n.
   For details see section 4.2.3
   For every successor m of n
       6.1 Compute g_m and h_m *[See section 4.2.2]*
       6.2 Compute f_m and insert m in OPEN.

7. **[ITERATE]**
   Goto [Step 2].

Generation of heuristics

The number of tracks required by a routing problem has been estimated by the *channel density* evaluated as follows. Let $L(N_j)$ and $R(N_j)$ denote the leftmost and rightmost columns respectively of the net N_j. Then:

$$Channel\ Density\ =\ max\{d_i \mid 1 \leq i \leq \#COL\}$$

where d_i denotes the number of nets N_j such that $L(N_j) \leq i \leq R(N_j)$ and $L(N_j) \neq R(N_j)$, and $\#COL$ is the number of columns (we assume that extra columns are not used).

An estimate of the number of vias required for a routing problem is obtained as follows:

$$\#vias\ =\ \sum_{i=1}^{\#nets} \#C_i$$

$\#C_i$ denotes the number of columns where net N_i has a terminal ($L(N_i) \neq R(N_i)$) and $\#nets$ is the number of nets to be routed.

4.2 The Channel Routing Problem

The estimate of the number of tracks, as well as the estimate of the number of vias are under-estimates, and therefore the heuristic vector computed using these estimates is admissible.

4.2.3 Selection of wires for a track

The scheme for generating the state space can be defined in different ways by adopting various strategies for selecting the combination of wires for a track. In this section we briefly describe the two greedy selection strategies used in our experiments. The selection schemes are derived from a greedy channel router proposed by Ho et al in [38].

The operations for the topmost track can be divided into the following phases:

- Assigning a set of non-overlapping wire segments on the track.
- Introduction of a set of vertical wire segments to connect the set of horizontal wire segments to the proper terminals at the top. Vertical wire segments also need to laid to define the top row of terminals for the new subproblem.
- Defining the new subproblem of routing the remaining wire segments in the lower tracks.

In general the vertical constraint graph corresponding to a problem instance may have cycles. In such cases doglegs must be introduced, but it is important to judiciously determine the position of these doglegs. It is preferable to introduce doglegs in columns with lower densities because each dogleg increases the density of the column by one. To implement this policy, an *acyclic vertical constraint graph* G_{avc} is constructed as follows.

- The set of vertices of G_{avc} is the same as that of G_{vc}.
- There is an edge from v_i to v_j iff:
    - There exists a column k such that net N_i has a terminal on the top of column k and net N_j has a terminal on the bottom of column k, and
    - There is no column k' with a density greater than that of column k such that net N_j has a terminal on the top of column k' and net N_i has a terminal on the bottom of column k.

To determine which wire segments are to be laid on the current topmost track, a parameter called *level* is computed for each net. The *level* of net N_i is defined as the length of the longest path from v_i to its descendant vertices in G_{avc}. The nets corresponding to nodes in G_{avc} with no incoming edges are called *free nets*.

It is easy to see that in the Manhattan model a wire segment W_i of net N_i can be laid on the topmost track provided both endpoints of the wire segment are in columns where the top terminal either belongs to N_i or is a non-terminal. Corresponding to each net N_i we define a set E_i of columns which can be endpoints to wire segments of N_i.

$$E_i = \{k \mid either\ T(k)\ is\ a\ terminal\ of\ N_i\ or\ a\ nonterminal\}$$

The greedy mechanisms used in our experiments for selecting wire segments for a track uses a hierarchy to determine the priority of the different wire segments. The hierarchy (proposed by Ho et al [38]) is as follows.

Def # 4.2 Feasible wires
A wire segment W_i of net N_i is a feasible wire segment if both endpoints of W_i are in columns belonging to the set E_i. □

Consider a feasible wire segment W_i of net N_i, which crosses a column k such that $B(k)$ is a terminal of N_i and $T(k)$ is a terminal of some other net. It is easy to see that W_i cannot be connected to the terminal $B(k)$ by a vertical wire segment in column k. Wire segments that do not intersect such columns are called *safe wires*.

Def # 4.3 Safe wires
A given feasible wire segment W_i is a safe wire if it does not intersect any column k where $B(k)$ is a terminal of net N_i and $T(k)$ is a terminal of some other net. □

Based on issues such as the vertical constraints and the density of the columns, a subset of *safe wires* have been classified as *optimal wires*.

Def # 4.4 Optimal wires
Consider the following sets of columns:

$$E_i^1 = \{k \mid k \in E_i,\ B(k)\ is\ a\ terminal\ of\ N_j\ other\ than\ N_i\ and\ level(N_i) > level(N_j)\} \bigcup \{k \mid k \in E_i,\ B(k)\ is\ a\ terminal\ of\ N_i\ or\ B(k) = 0\}$$

$$E_i^2 = \{k \mid k \in E_i,\ k = L(N_i)\ or\ k = R(N_i)\ or\ d_k < d_{max}\}$$

$$E_i^3 = \{k \mid k \in E_i,\ L(N_i) \leq k \leq R(N_i)\}$$

$$E_i^* = E_i^1 \cap E_i^2 \cap E_i^3$$

A given safe wire S_i is an optimal wire if both endpoints of the wire are in columns belonging to E_i^*. □

While the above hierarchy has been used by one of the greedy mechanisms for selecting the wires for a track, the other greedy selection scheme (whose primary concern is to minimize the number of doglegs) attempts to assign *full wires* whenever possible. *Full wires* are defined as follows.

4.2 The Channel Routing Problem

Def # 4.5 Full wires
A given optimal wire O_i is a full wire if it covers the entire span of net N_i. □

Of the two greedy selection schemes used in our experiments, the first uses the greedy routing algorithm *MCRP_ROUT* of Ho et al [38]. The steps is selecting the wire segments are as follows:

1. Select the set H_o of non-overlapping optimal wires from the high density columns to lower density columns, giving first priority to wires of *free nets* and secondly to wires of maximal span. If the selected set H_o does not cover all the columns having maximum density then continue selecting alternate sets of optimal wires until either a set H_o^* is found that covers all the columns of maximum density, or all possibilities are exhausted.

2. If the set of wires in H_o^* does not cover all the columns of maximum density, then set $H_o^* \leftarrow \phi$.

3. Assign non-overlapping feasible wires on the topmost track as follows:

    (a) If the length of the longest path in G_{avc} is greater than or equal to the channel density, then introduce a set of wire segments to minimize the length of the longest path in G_{avc}.

    (b) Introduce a set of wire segments to maximize the number of free nets.

The primary concern of the above selection scheme is to minimize the number of tracks. The second greedy selection scheme used in our experiments attempts to minimize the number of doglegs while choosing the wire segments. The steps for selecting wires for this combination are as follows:

1. Select the set H_f of non-overlapping full wires from the high density columns to lower density columns, giving first priority to wires of *free nets* and secondly to wires of maximal span. If the selected set H_f does not cover all the columns having maximum density then continue selecting alternate sets of full wires until either a set H_f^* is found that covers all the columns of maximum density, or all possibilities are exhausted.

2. If the set of wires in H_f^* does not cover all the columns of maximum density, then select that set of non-overlapping full wires (from the alternate sets discovered earlier) that covers most of the columns of maximum density.

Since greedy schemes are used to select the combination of wire segments for a track, the channel router is not guaranteed to find solutions that are non-dominated in the entire search space. However the algorithm MObj_Route finds the set of non-dominated solutions in the portion of the state space defined by the two greedy selection schemes. We shall later see that the policy is quite useful in benchmark problem instances like the Deutsch difficult problem.

A typical solution obtained by our approach will have some tracks where the combination of wires selected by the first scheme have been used while the second scheme have been used on the other tracks. The tracks in which the first combination have been used are likely to contain many more broken nets than necessary. Since it is impossible to determine a priori which of these wire segments can be accommodated with the remaining portion of the corresponding nets in lower tracks, we have used a simple post processing step to reduce the fragmentation of nets.

The experimental results on the channel routing problem is presented in section 4.4. In that section we also compare the performance of the algorithm MObj_Route with straightforward extensions of well known single objective search approaches.

4.3 The Log Cutting problem

The log-cutting problem (also known as the roll-cutting problem) is a variant of the bin-packing problem [29]. The basic problem is as follows.

- A log cutting shop delivers slices of logs. The logs are of similar length, but the length of the slices vary according to the orders received by the shop.

- A log is cut by a set of blades which descend simultaneously and orthogonally on the log. Depending on the length of the slices in which a log is to be cut, the position of the blades are arranged, and the whole log is sliced all at once. The position of the blades therefore determine the *cutting pattern* of the log.

- Adjusting the position of the blades is a time consuming process. Obviously, logs requiring the same *cutting pattern* can be sliced successively without moving the blades.

- Given a set of orders for slices of various sizes, the dual objective of the *log cutting problem* is to optimize the *number of logs* required to deliver all the orders and the *number of distinct cutting patterns* (so that minimum number of adjustments of the position of the blades is required).

The state space of the problem is a tree where the root node represents the given problem where all the ordered slices have to be allocated to the logs. Every other non-terminal node represents a partially solved subproblem of the original problem, where some of the slices have been allocated to some logs and the remaining slices are yet to be allocated. The goal nodes are those where all the slices have been allocated to logs.

Expansion of a node is equivalent to allocating all slices of a particular size to one or more logs, and generating separate children for each possible allocation. Each child node represents a distinct partially solved subproblem of allocating the remaining slices.

The heuristic cost vector of a node is evaluated as follows.

Number of logs: Any slice that remains to be allocated and can fit into the left-over portion of any log are assumed to be allocated. Thus if L denotes the length of the largest left-over from any log, then all slices of length less than L that remain to be allocated are assumed to be allocated. The sum of the length of the other remaining slices divided by the log-size gives a lower bound on the number of logs still required.

Number of cutting patterns: The sum of the lengths of each slice of distinct length that remains to be allocated divided by the log-size gives a lower bound on the number of cutting patterns required.

The method of obtaining the heuristic estimate for the number of logs required may seem a bit naive. However since the heuristic obtained in this manner is non-monotonic in nature, it has been used to evaluate the amount of reduction in node expansions by using the *pathmax* property described in chapter 3.

It is easy to see that a more elegant estimate of the number of logs may be obtained as follows. Instead of assuming that all slices whose lengths are less than the maximum left-over length L are allocated, the number of slices that can actually fit in the left-over lengths is evaluated. Then the sum of the length of the other remaining slices divided by the log-size gives a stronger lower bound on the number of logs still required.

In the following section we present the experimental results of the problems considered in this section and the preceding two sections. The results are also used to compare the basic multiobjective search strategies with obvious extensions of well known single objective search schemes.

4.4 Evaluation of the Multiobjective Strategies

The algorithms presented in this chapter have been applied on randomly generated problem instances. In almost all problem instances competitive multiple non-dominated solutions were obtained. Since the operator scheduling problem and the channel routing problem are of great practical significance, we present the solution sets obtained for some of the instances of this problem in tables 4.1 and 4.2 respectively.

The random graph generator used for generating instances of the operator scheduling problem accepts a 4-tuple denoted by (n_1, n_2, n_3, n_4) where n_1 specifies the critical number of time steps, n_2 specifies the maximum number of operations in a time step of the ASAP schedule of the graph, n_3 specifies the maximum number of parents of any operation and n_4 specifies the maximum number of operation types. The random generator uses an uniform random distribution to construct a DFG which meets the given specifications.

The random generator used to generate netlists for the channel routing problem takes three inputs, namely the number of nets, the number of columns in the channel, and the number of terminals in the channel. The algorithm MObj_Route was also applied to the *Deutsch difficult channel* which is a well known benchmark for channel routers. In table 4.2 we have presented the solutions obtained by MObj_Route for this channel. We also present (in Fig 4.5) a 19 track solution for this channel that uses 327 vias (of which

#	Graph Pmts	#θ	Solutions
1.	<5,4,4,4>	15	(5,5),(4,6)
2.	<4,3,3,3>	7	(4,4),(3,5)
3.	<6,5,5,5>	21	(9,6),(7,7),(6,8),(5,9)
4.	<7,5,5,5>	25	(10,7),(8,8),(7,9),(6,10),(5,11)
5.	<5,6,5,5>	11	(6,5),(5,6),(4,8)
6.	<7,7,7,7>	31	(12,7),(9,8),(8,9),(7,10)

#θ: Number of operations in the DFG.
Solutions: (number of operators, number of time steps)

Table 4.1: Results of MObj_Schedule

Channel	Density	Solutions
Deutsch Diff.	19	(19,35),(20,18),(21,11),(22,8)
exp2	18	(18,33),(19,24)
exp3	22	(22,19),(23,16),(25,13),(26,10)
exp4	14	(14,12),(15,6),(16,2),(17,0)
exp5	15	(15,38),(16,20),(17,18)

Solutions: (number of tracks, number of additional vias due to doglegs)

Table 4.2: Results of MObj_Route

35 are additional vias in the form of doglegs) and no net detours outside its span. To the best of our knowledge this is the best solution of this problem for routing within net boundaries.

In this section we compare the performance of the multiobjective search strategies presented in chapter 3 with other strategies. The experimental results reported in this section are those obtained by applying the extensions of the algorithms of chapter 3 on the problems described in this chapter. For example, MOA^{**} is equivalent to MObj_Schedule for the operator scheduling problem and MObj_Route for the channel routing problem. Also the results are for the same set of problem instances as in tables 4.1 and 4.2.

The results obtained by running the multiobjective search strategies have been compared with the results of running straight-forward extensions of A^* and $DFBB$ on the same problem instances. The extended algorithms are as follows.

- **ItrA*:** This is an extension of A^* where one criteria is iteratively optimized for different values of the other dimensions. For example, in the Scheduling problem A^* is applied iteratively to optimize the total operator area for various given number of time steps. Likewise, in the Channel routing problem, A^* is applied to optimize the number of doglegs for different channel widths.

- **DFBB:** The Depth-first Branch and Bound strategy can be easily extended to the multiobjective framework as follows. Search proceeds depth first and at each node

4.4 Evaluation of the Multiobjective Strategies

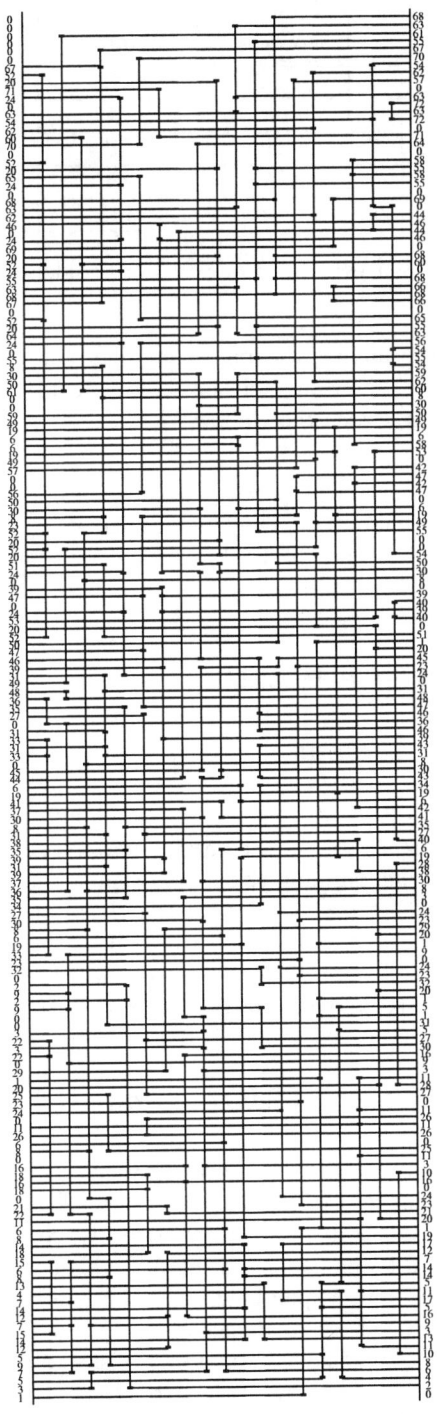

Figure 4.5: Solution of the Deutsch Difficult Channel obtained by MObj_Route

#	Number of orders	Nodes with $pathmax$	Nodes without $pathmax$
1.	23	20	21
2.	27	21	24
3.	29	18	25
4.	59	84	217
5.	62	325	1031

Table 4.3: Results of Log Cutting Problem: $pathmax$ vs $no\ pathmax$

the successor having the minimum non-dominated representative cost vector is visited first. When any solution is found, its cost vector becomes another upper bound on the search that follows.

In the following subsections we present experimental results related to some of the issues discussed in chapter 3. They include the utility of $pathmax$ for searching with non-monotonic heuristics, and the backing-up of multiple cost vectors in memory bounded search.

4.4.1 Utility of $Pathmax$

The non-monotonic heuristic described in section 4.3 was used by MOMA*0 to solve instances of the Log Cutting Problem. Table 4.3 shows the number of nodes expanded by MOMA*0 when it uses $pathmax$ besides the number of nodes expanded when it does not use $pathmax$. Since the same heuristic function and cost backup mechanism is used in both cases, the actual running times are proportional to the number of nodes expanded by each of them. The results reflect the expected benefit of $pathmax$ for searching using non-monotone heuristics. The number of nodes indicated in table 4.3 are the number of nodes expanded by the algorithm. Due to a large branching factor, the number of nodes actually generated is extremely large, rendering it infeasible to use MOA^{**} for the LCP.

4.4.2 Comparison of MOA** and ItrA*

Table 4.4 shows the number of nodes expanded by $DFBB$, $ItrA^*$ and MOA^{**} on the same problem instances of the Channel Routing Problem as in table 4.2. We have also included the DFBB strategy for comparison to show that in some cases (as in $exp2$) DFBB may expand fewer nodes than ItrA*. This is because DFBB expands a node only once whereas ItrA* may expand the same node in more than one iteration. The actual running times of the three strategies is proportional to the number of nodes expanded by each of them because node expansions take significant amount of time and the total number of nodes expanded by MOA^{**} or $ItrA^*$ is not very large for the overhead of selection to be significant over DFBB.

4.4 Evaluation of the Multiobjective Strategies

Channel	Density	DFBB	ItrA*	MOA**
Deutsch diff.	19	10228	4962	4056
exp2	18	9292	10142	6710
exp3	22	12023	5655	2876
exp4	14	1195	242	202
exp5	15	1083	727	289

Table 4.4: Number of nodes expanded in the Channel Routing Problem

#	Graph Prmts	#θ	MOA**	ItrA*
1.	$<5,4,4,4>$	15	25	30
2.	$<4,3,3,3>$	7	12	14
3.	$<6,5,5,5>$	21	62	87
4.	$<7,5,5,5>$	25	270	365
5.	$<5,6,5,5>$	11	26	41
6.	$<7,7,7,7>$	31	109	189

#θ: Number of operations in the data flow graph.

Table 4.5: Nodes expanded by MOA** and ItrA* in the Operator Scheduling Problem

Table 4.5 presents the comparison of nodes expanded by MOA** and ItrA* on the same instances of the Operator Scheduling Problem as those in table 4.1. The ratio of the number of nodes expanded by the strategies also reflects the ratio of their actual running times.

The results shown in tables 4.4 and 4.5 show that MOA^{**} is superior to $ItrA^*$ and $DFBB$ in terms of the number of nodes expanded (which is commensurate with the actual running times in our experiments). This reflects the advantage of a single best-first exploration of the multiobjective state space over multiple iterative searches (as in $ItrA^*$) and depth-first branch and bound.

4.4.3 Comparison of MOMA*0 and DFBB

The relative performance of the linear space strategies MOMA*0 and DFBB is shown in table 4.6. The results are for the same instances of the Operator Scheduling Problem as those depicted in table 4.1.

Table 4.6 shows that though MOMA*0 typically has to re-expand nodes, it expands fewer nodes than DFBB. This shows that the number of dominated nodes expanded by DFBB is usually more than the number of nodes regenerated by MOMA*0 justifying the *best-first* policy adopted by MOMA*0.

#	Graph Prmts	#θ	MOMA*0	DFBB
1.	$< 5, 4, 4, 4 >$	15	30	43
2.	$< 4, 3, 3, 3 >$	7	14	16
3.	$< 6, 5, 5, 5 >$	21	87	104
4.	$< 7, 5, 5, 5 >$	25	362	391
5.	$< 5, 6, 5, 5 >$	11	46	58
6.	$< 7, 7, 7, 7 >$	31	185	227

#θ: Number of operations in the data flow graph.

Table 4.6: Nodes expanded by MOMA*0 and DFBB in the Operator Scheduling Problem

#	No. of orders	MOMA*0		MOMA*N	
		Nodes	Calls	Nodes	Calls
1.	23	12	1770	9	1753
2.	27	12	1995	9	1988
3.	29	12	3102	9	3093
4.	59	34	39762	29	39214
5.	62	284	546251	261	544213

Table 4.7: Results of Log Cutting Problem: Single vs Multiple back-up costs

4.4.4 Effect of multiple back-up costs in MOMA*0

In this section we present results from the Log Cutting Problem and the Operator Scheduling Problem to illustrate the advantages and drawbacks of backing-up multiple cost vectors in memory bounded search.

Table 4.7 shows the number of nodes expanded by MOMA*0 and its variant (called MOMA*N) which backs up the entire non-dominated set of cost vectors from the pruned space. In these experiments on the Log Cutting Problem we have used the more computationally expensive monotonic heuristic function described in section 4.3. The number of calls to the heuristic function is also shown in table 4.7.

Since only one heuristic cost vector is evaluated at each node of LCP, the number of calls to the heuristic function actually reflects the number of nodes generated. The heuristic evaluation being costly, the number of calls to the heuristic function dictates the actual running time of each strategy. The results demonstrate the superiority of MOMA*N over MOMA*0 in the LCP problem.

While the results shown in table 4.7 reflect the advantage of backing up multiple cost vectors, table 4.8 presents results on the Operator Scheduling Problem that illustrate the drawbacks of this policy. Since the heuristic function used for the Operator Scheduling Problem is also computationally expensive the number of calls to the heuristic function is a better criterion for comparing the strategies MOMA*0 and MOMA*N. In table 4.8 we also present results for the strategy MOMA*2 which is a variant of $MOMA^*0$ that

4.4 Evaluation of the Multiobjective Strategies

hline #	No. of Opns.	MOMA*0 Nodes	MOMA*0 Calls	MOMA*2 Nodes	MOMA*2 Calls	MOMA*N Nodes	MOMA*N Calls
1.	15	30	53	29	77	25	532
2.	7	14	23	13	33	12	69
3.	21	87	184	85	268	78	1062
4.	25	362	721	358	1392	340	22450
5.	11	46	122	38	195	30	436
6.	31	185	431	182	818	143	12171

Table 4.8: Results of Operator Scheduling Problem: Single vs Multiple back-up costs

backs up the minimum *two* cost vectors (in K-order) while backtracking.

Since it is possible to generate multiple cost vectors at every node in the state space of the Operator Scheduling Problem, and MOMA*N computes each of these vectors, the number of calls to the heuristic function by MOMA*N is much more than that of $MOMA*0$ which computes only the representative cost vector of a node at the time of its generation. This is reflected in table 4.8 which shows that MOMA*0 is more efficient than MOMA*N in such situations. The performance of $MOMA*2$ is between these strategies indicating the scope of tradeoff between the number of cost vectors that have to be backed up with the number of nodes that have to be re-generated.

Chapter 5

Multiobjective Problem Reduction Search

Problem reduction search is a popular scheme for solving problems that can be hierarchically broken down to a conjunction or disjunction of subproblems [69]. Since such problems can be conveniently represented by AND/OR graphs, problem reduction search is often considered to be synonymous with the problem of searching AND/OR graphs. The algorithm AO^* is the most well studied strategy for this representation [11, 41, 62, 63, 68, 69].

Popular best-first strategies (such as AO^*) adopt the policy of expanding only those nodes that belong to *potential solution graphs* (*psg*s) whose cost is less than or equal to the cost of the optimal solution graph. This is ensured by expanding only nodes belonging to the current minimum cost *psg* in the explicit AND/OR graph. Since the task of identifying the minimum cost *psg* in an explicit single objective additive AND/OR graph is polynomial in the number of nodes in the graph, the complexity of AO^* is polynomial in the number of nodes it expands.

A natural approach would be to extend this policy to the multiobjective search framework, where only nodes belonging to non-dominated *psg*s are expanded. However, in this study[1] we have been able to establish the following major result which shows that the multiobjective search problem differs from the conventional problem in one of the basic aspects.

- Given an explicit additive multiobjective AND/OR graph, the task of identifying a non-dominated cost potential solution graph (*psg*) is NP-hard in general.

---

[1] Reprinted from *Journal of Algorithms*, 20, Dasgupta, Chakrabarti, DeSarkar, *Multiobjective Heuristic Search in AND/OR graphs*, 282-311, 1996, with permission from Academic Press

The result implies that the polynomial time marking strategy of AO^* cannot be extended to the multiobjective framework unless $P = NP$. In view of this we have investigated the task of developing effective strategies for the multiobjective problem. Taking a different approach we present a linear space AND/OR graph search strategy called $MObj^*$ and analyze its properties.

This chapter also presents other results on multiobjective search of AND/OR graphs. In particular, we show that the use of an induced total ordering such as *K-ordering* (defined in chapter 3) is essential for identifying a non-dominated cost *psg*. The issues related to selection using *pathmax* have also been considered.

The chapter is organized as follows. In section 5.1 we present the preliminary definitions and a formal definition of the problem of multiobjective search of AND/OR graphs. The sections 5.2, 5.3 and 5.4 describe the main difficulties in the selection of non-dominated cost *psgs*. Section 5.2 shows that the use of an induced total ordering such as *K-ordering* is essential for identifying a non-dominated cost *psg* in the explicit AND/OR graph. In section 5.3 we show that when the heuristic function is non-monotonic the task of selection using *pathmax* is NP-hard. The most important result of this chapter which establishes that in general the task of selection is NP-hard even when the heuristics are monotone is presented in section 5.4. Section 5.5 presents the strategy $MObj^*$ and analyzes its properties.

5.1 The problem definition

The problem of multiobjective AND/OR graph search differs from the conventional problem mainly in the cost structure. This section describes the cost structure of the multiobjective problem and presents the preliminary definitions. The basic problem can be stated as follows:

> **The Multiobjective AND/OR Graph Search Problem:**
> **Given :**
>   1. The search space, represented as a locally-finite directed AND/OR graph.
>   2. A single start node in the graph.
>   3. A set of terminal (or solved) nodes in the graph.
>   4. A positive vector valued cost associated with each arc in the graph.
>   5. A heuristic function that returns a set of vectors at each node.
>
> **To Find :**
>   The set of non-dominated solution graphs in the search-space graph.

The structure of an AND/OR graph and the properties of AND-nodes and OR-nodes have been described in detail in Nilsson's book [69]. We restrict ourselves to the definitions that are characteristic to the multiobjective representation and those which are necessary for conveying the notation used throughout this chapter.

5.1 The problem definition

The definitions of *dominance* and *K-ordering* have been presented in the chapters 2 and 3 respectively. Throughout this chapter we assume that the number of dimensions of the problem is K, and therefore all cost vectors have K-dimensions. The definitions of the vector operators $+$ and $-$, and the vector max-function $vmax()$ follow from chapter 3.

Problem reduction search approaches generally assume that an implicit specification of the AND/OR graph representing the search space is given. During the course of search various portions of the search space AND/OR graph is generated (or made explicit) by the search strategy. Let G denote the implicit state-space AND/OR graph. A solution graph D(m) rooted at node m is a subgraph of G with the following properties:

Solution Graph: D(m)
1. Node m is in D(m).
2. If n is an OR-node in G, and n is in D(m), then exactly one of its immediate successors in G is in D(m).
3. If n is an AND-node in G and n is in D(m), then all its immediate successors in G are in D(m).
4. Every tip node in D(m) (that is, nodes with no children) is a terminal (solved) node.
5. No node other than m and its descendants in G are in D(m).

A *potential solution graph* (*psg*) is a subgraph of the *explicit* AND/OR graph, whose definition is similar to that of a solution graph except that the tip nodes of a *psg* are not necessarily terminal (or solved) nodes of the search-space graph G, but they must be tip nodes of the explicit AND/OR graph.

In the multiobjective framework each edge of an AND/OR graph has a *cost vector*. Each dimension of the edge cost vector represents the cost of decomposing the parent problem along that dimension. Every terminal node n in the search space has a cost vector $t(n)$ which represents the (vector valued) cost of solving the primitive problem represented by n. The cost vector of a solution graph $D(m)$ rooted at a node m is recursively computed as follows using the sumcost criteria:

Cost vector of Solution Graph: C[D(m)]
1. If m is a terminal node then $C[D(m)] = t(m)$
2. If m is an OR-node with immediate successor n in $D(m)$, then
$$C[D(m)] = c(m,n) + C[D(n)]$$
where $c(m,n)$ denotes the cost vector of the edge from m to n.
3. If m is an AND-node with the set of immediate successors $n_1, \ldots, n_J$, then
$$C[D(m)] = \sum_{i=1}^{J}(c(m,n_i) + C[D(n_i)])$$

In the above computation every addition refers to dimension-wise addition of the cost vectors as defined for the $+$ operator in chapter 3. A solution graph is said to be non-dominated if its cost vector is non-dominated.

Note that if we use such a recursive computation of costs, then for every node n in the solution graph $D(m)$, $(n \neq m)$, the cost $C[D(n)]$ is added to every parent of the node n in $D(m)$. This scheme of cost computation is popularly known as *additive cost computation* and the corresponding search problem is called the problem of searching *additive AND/OR graphs*. Throughout this study, we consider the problem of searching additive AND/OR graphs.

In the multiobjective framework, we may have several mutually non-dominated solution graphs rooted at each node n. Consequently the heuristic evaluation function will typically return a set $H(n)$ of non-dominated heuristic vectors at the node n, such that each vector $h(n)$ in $H(n)$ estimates the cost vector of one or more solution graphs rooted at n. At every terminal node n, $H(n)$ contains the single cost vector $t(n)$. The definitions of *admissible* and *monotone* heuristics are as follows.

Def # 5.1 Admissible heuristics:
A multiobjective heuristic function is said to be admissible if the set $H(n)$ of heuristic vectors computed at each node n satisfies the following property:

Admissibility property: *For every solution graph $D(n)$ rooted at the node n, there exists a heuristic vector $h(n)$ in $H(n)$ such that $h(n)$ either dominates the cost vector $C[D(n)]$ of $D(n)$ or is equal to it.*

It should be noted that in one extreme case $H(n)$ may contain a single vector which satisfies the above property, while in the other extreme case $H(n)$ may contain a distinct cost vector corresponding to each solution graph rooted at n. □

Def # 5.2 Monotone heuristics:
A multiobjective heuristic evluation function is said to be monotone (or consistent) if it satisfies the following properties for all nodes in the search space:

1. *If node n_i is a successor of an OR-node n then for each heuristic vector $h(n_i)$ in $H(n_i)$, there exists a heuristic vector $h(n)$ in $H(n)$, such that $h(n)$ either dominates the cost vector $c(n, n_i) + h(n_i)$ or is equal to it.*

2. *If nodes $n_1, \ldots, n_M$ are the successors of an AND-node n then for every choice of $h(n_i)$ from $H(n_i)$, there exists $h(n)$ in $H(n)$ such that $h(n)$ either dominates the cost vector $\sum_{i=1}^{M}(c(n, n_i) + h(n_i))$, or is equal to it.* □

Since the non-terminal tip nodes of a *psg* may have multiple heuristic vectors it follows that a *psg* will typically have a set of non-dominated cost vectors that estimate the different solution graphs of which the *psg* is a subgraph. The set of non-dominated cost vectors $F[D'(n)]$ of a given *psg* $D'(n)$ is recursively computed as follows:

Set of cost vectors of a psg: $F[D'(n)]$
1. If n is a tip node then $F[D'(n)] = H(n)$
2. If n is an OR-node with immediate successor m in $D(n)$, then
$$F[D'(n)] = ND\{c(n, m) + f[D'(m)], \quad \forall f[D'(m)] \in F[D'(m)]\}$$

where $c(n, m)$ is the cost of the edge from n to m, and $D'(m)$ denotes the subgraph of $D'(n)$ which is rooted at the successor m of n.

3. If n is an AND-node with set of immediate successors $m_1, \ldots, m_J$, then
$$F[D'(n)] = ND\{\sum_{i=1}^{J}(c(n, m_i) + f[D'(m_i)]), \quad \forall f[D'(m_i)] \in F[D'(m_i)]\}$$
where each $D'(m_i)$ denotes the subgraph of $D'(n)$ which is rooted at the successor m_i of n.

In the above definition $ND\{Y\}$ denotes the non-dominated subset of a given set $\{Y\}$. A given *psg* is said to be non-dominated if one or more of its cost vectors are non-dominated. A *maximal non-dominated psg* is defined as follows.

Def # 5.3 Maximal non-dominated psg:
A *psg* $D'(s)$ *(rooted at the start node s), of some explicit graph of the implicit search space is said to be a maximal non-dominated psg if:*

1. *There exists a vector $f[D'(s)] \in F[D'(s)]$ such that $f[D'(s)]$ is non-dominated by every solution graph in the search space, and,*

2. *No other psg (of any explicit graph in the search space) which is rooted at s and is a subgraph of $D'(s)$ has a cost $f[D'(s)]$.*

□

The set of cost vectors $F(n)$ at a node n is defined as follows:
$$F(n) = ND\left\{\bigcup F[D'(n)], \quad \forall \text{ psgs } D'(n) \text{ in the explicit graph}\right\}$$

In the multiobjective problem an OR-node may have multiple non-dominated successors defined as follows.

Def # 5.4 Non-dominated successors of an OR-node:
A successor n_i of an OR-node n is a non-dominated successor if there exists at least one cost vector $f(n_i)$ in $F(n_i)$, such that the cost vector $c(n, n_i) + f(n_i)$ is non-dominated by every cost vector of the form $c(n, n_j) + f(n_j)$ where n_j is a different successor of n and $f(n_j) \in F(n_j)$. □

5.2 The utility of K-ordering

Best-first strategies for searching AND/OR graphs typically execute three basic steps in each iteration. In strategies such as AO^* the first step in each iteration is to select the minimum cost *psg* in the explicit AND/OR graph. The next step is to expand a non-terminal tip node of the *psg* and generate the successors of that node. The third major task of AO^* is to perform a cost revision of the psgs.

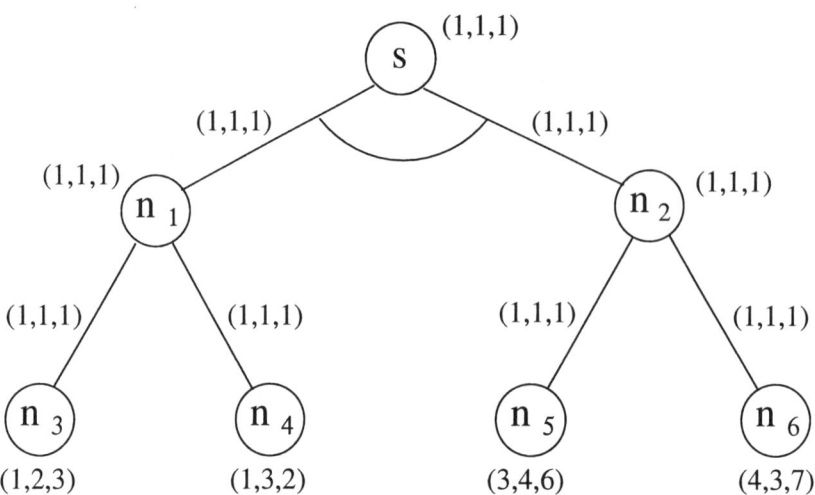

Figure 5.1: AND/OR graph illustrating the utility of K-ordering

AO^* uses a simple effective scheme for identifying the minimum cost *psg* in the explicit graph. It employs a marking mechanism [69] such that every successor of AND-nodes and the minimum cost successor of OR-nodes are marked. This marking policy ensures that the marked *psg* rooted at the start node s is the one having minimum cost.

A natural way of extending this scheme to the multiobjective framework would be to select *non-dominated successors* (as defined in section 5.1) of OR-nodes. It is easy to see that the necessary condition for a *psg* to be non-dominated is that the successor of each OR-node will have to be a non-dominated successor. Is the same condition sufficient for a *psg* to be non-dominated? The following example shows that the answer is negative. To convey the result in simple terms we have chosen an example where each tip node has a single cost vector.

Example # 5.1 Let us consider the explicit graph in Fig 5.1. Both successors of the OR-nodes n_1 and n_2 are non-dominated. If we select the successor n_4 from n_1 and the successor n_6 from n_2, then the resulting *psg* $[s, n_1, n_2, n_4, n_6]$ has the single cost vector (9,10,13). Instead, if we select the other successors from both n_1 and n_2, then the *psg* $[s, n_1, n_2, n_3, n_5]$ has the cost vector (8,10,13) which dominates the previous *psg*. □

This shows that an arbitrary choice of non-dominated successors of OR-nodes is not sufficient to guarantee that the *psg* will be non-dominated. One way to resolve this issue is to impose an induced total order on the cost vectors and select the minimum cost successor of every OR-node based on that total order. For example, if we use the K-ordering described in chapter 3 then in the graph in Fig 5.1 we shall select the successor n_3 from node n_1 and the successor n_5 from node n_2. In the more general case, where each of the successors $n_1, \ldots, n_J$ of an OR-node n can have multiple non-dominated cost vectors, we select the successor n_i for which the following vector is minimum in K-order:

$$c(n, n_i) + kmin\{h(n_i), \forall h(n_i) \in H(n_i)\}$$

The function *kmin* returns the minimum vector in K-order from a set of vectors. It is easy to see that the total order ensures that the *psg* identified in this manner will have the minimum cost vector in K-order, and therefore will be non-dominated.

5.3 Selection using *pathmax* is NP-hard

We have shown in chapter 3 that *pathmax* has a special significance in multiobjective state space search since it is useful in non-pathological problem instances as well. In this section we first demonstrate the way in which *pathmax* can be used in multiobjective search of AND/OR graphs and show that the standard benefit of *pathmax* extends to this problem. Finally we present the most important result of this section which states that the task of selecting a non-dominated cost *psg* using *pathmax* is NP-hard.

Def # 5.5 Cost of psg using pathmax:
At every tip node n in the explicit graph, the set of cost vectors using pathmax is the same as $H(n)$. For every non-tip OR-node n of the given psg, the set of cost vectors using pathmax (denoted by $F(n)$) can be recursively computed (as follows) from the set of cost vectors $F(n_i)$, where n_i is the successor of n in the psg:

- For each $h(n) \in H(n)$ and $f(n_i) \in F(n_i)$
    Set $f(n) \leftarrow vmax\{h(n), f(n_i) + c(n, n_i)\}$
    Put $f(n)$ in $F(n)$
- Remove dominated vectors from $F(n)$

The function $vmax\{\vec{x}, \vec{y}\}$ returns a vector which is equal to the maximum of $\vec{x}$ and $\vec{y}$ in each dimension. For every non-tip AND-node n with successors $n_1, \ldots, n_J$, the set of cost vectors $F(n)$ using pathmax can be recursively computed as follows:

- For each $h(n) \in H(n)$ and $f(n_i) \in F(n_i)$, $1 \leq i \leq J$
    Set $f(n) \leftarrow vmax\{h(n), \sum_{i=1}^{J}(f(n_i) + c(n, n_i))\}$
    Put $f(n)$ in $F(n)$
- Remove dominated vectors from $F(n)$

It is easy to see that the cost vector of solution graphs is not affected by pathmax. □

The following example illustrates the utility of *pathmax* in terms of the number of node expansions. For simplicity we have chosen an example where every node has a single cost vector.

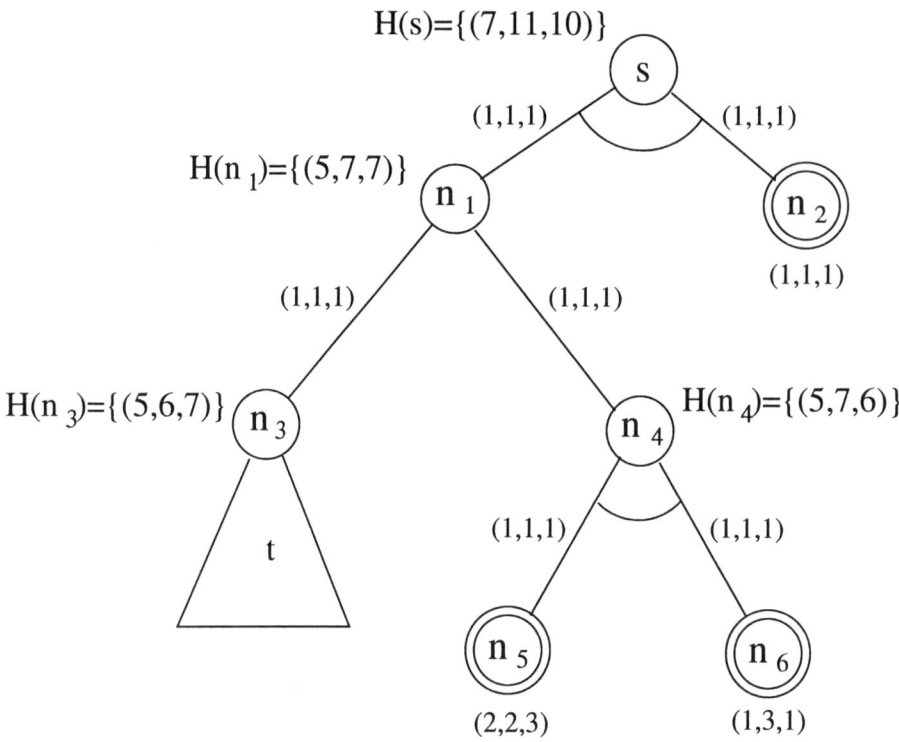

Figure 5.2: AND/OR graph illustrating the utility of pathmax

Example # 5.2 Let us consider the explicit AND/OR graph shown in Fig 5.2. t represents the (implicit) portion of the search-space graph rooted at n_3. If the cost vectors are evaluated without pathmax, then the *psg* consisting of the nodes $[s, n_1, n_2, n_3]$ has the sole cost vector $(9,10,11)$, which is inconsistent with the heuristic vector $(7,11,10)$ of node s. In the explicit graph we have only one other *psg* $[s, n_1, n_2, n_4, n_5, n_6]$ which has a cost vector $(9,11,10)$. The latter is also a solution graph.

If we do not use pathmax, then the cost vector of the psg $[s, n_1, n_2, n_3]$ is non-dominated by the cost vector of every solution graph in the search space. Therefore the *psg* will be extended further through the expansion of node n_3 and possibly other nodes in t. However if pathmax is used, then the cost vector of the psg $[s, n_1, n_2, n_3]$ will be revised to $(9,11,11)$, which is consistent with the heuristic vector at the node s. The revised cost vector is dominated by the cost vector of the solution graph $[s, n_1, n_2, n_4, n_5, n_6]$, and therefore neither n_3 nor any other node in t will be expanded. □

The following theorem establishes the correctness of *pathmax*.

Theorem # 5.1 *If the heuristic function is admissible, then the cost vectors computed using pathmax are also admissible.*

5.3 Selection using pathmax

Proof: The cost vectors at the tip-nodes remain the same using *pathmax* (by definition). We show that the set of cost vectors $F(n)$ computed at a node n using *pathmax* is admissible if the set of cost vectors $F(n_i)$ at each successor n_i of n is admissible. The result then follows by induction.

Let $D(n)$ be a solution graph rooted at an OR-node n. Let n_i be the successor of n in $D(n)$. Let $D(n_i)$ denote the solution graph rooted at n_i which is a subgraph of $D(n)$. Thus:

$$C[D(n)] = C[D(n_i)] + c(n, n_i)$$

Since $F(n_i)$ is admissible, there exists a cost vector $f(n_i)$ in $F(n_i)$ such that $f(n_i)$ dominates the cost vector of $D(n_i)$ or is equal to it. Therefore, $f(n_i) + c(n, n_i)$ dominates $C[D(n)]$. Since $H(n)$ is admissible, therefore there exists a vector $h(n)$ in $H(n)$ such that $h(n)$ dominates $C[D(n)]$ or is equal to it. It is easy to see that the dimension-wise maximum of $h(n)$ and the vector $f(n) + c(n, n_i)$ will also dominate $C[D(n)]$. It follows that $F(n)$ is admissible.

Let $D(n)$ be a solution graph rooted at an AND-node n. Let $n_1, \ldots, n_J$ be the successors of n. Let $D(n_i)$ denote the solution graph rooted at successor n_i which is a subgraph of $D(n)$. Thus:

$$C[D(n)] = \sum_{i=1}^{J} C[D(n_i)] + c(n, n_i)$$

Since each $F(n_i)$ is admissible, there exists $f(n_i)$ in $F(n_i)$ such that $f(n_i)$ dominates the cost vector of $D(n_i)$ or is equal to it. Therefore, $\sum_{i=1}^{J}(f(n_i) + c(n, n_i))$ dominates $C[D(n)]$. Since $H(n)$ is admissible, therefore there exists a vector $h(n)$ in $H(n)$ such that $h(n)$ dominates $C[D(n)]$ or is equal to it. It is easy to see that the dimension-wise maximum of $h(n)$ and the vector $\sum_{i=1}^{J}(f(n_i) + c(n, n_i))$ will also dominate $C[D(n)]$. It follows that $F(n)$ is admissible. □

Theorem 5.1 and example 5.2 show that when the heuristic function is non-monotonic the set of cost vectors of a *psg* should be computed using *pathmax*. We now show that when the set of cost vectors of *psgs* are evaluated using *pathmax* the task of identifying a non-dominated cost *psg* is NP-hard.

Theorem # 5.2 *Given an explicit AND/OR graph, identifying a non-dominated psg is NP-hard if the cost vectors are computed using pathmax.*

Proof: We show that any instance of the integer set partition problem can be reduced to a two-objective instance of the given problem. The integer set partition problem requires us to find a partition P of a given set $A = \{a_1, a_2, \ldots, a_M\}$ of M positive integers, such that:

$$\sum_{i \in P} a_i = \sum_{i \notin P} a_i$$

In other words, if S denotes the sum of all the integers in A, then the task is to identify a partition P whose sum is $S/2$. The integer set partition problem is known to be NP-hard [41].

Given an instance of the integer set partition problem, we construct an AND/OR graph in the following way. The root node s is an AND-node with children $n_1, n_2, \ldots, n_M$ (see Fig 5.3). Each node n_i is an OR-node with two children n_i^1 and n_i^2. Node n_i^1 has a single cost vector

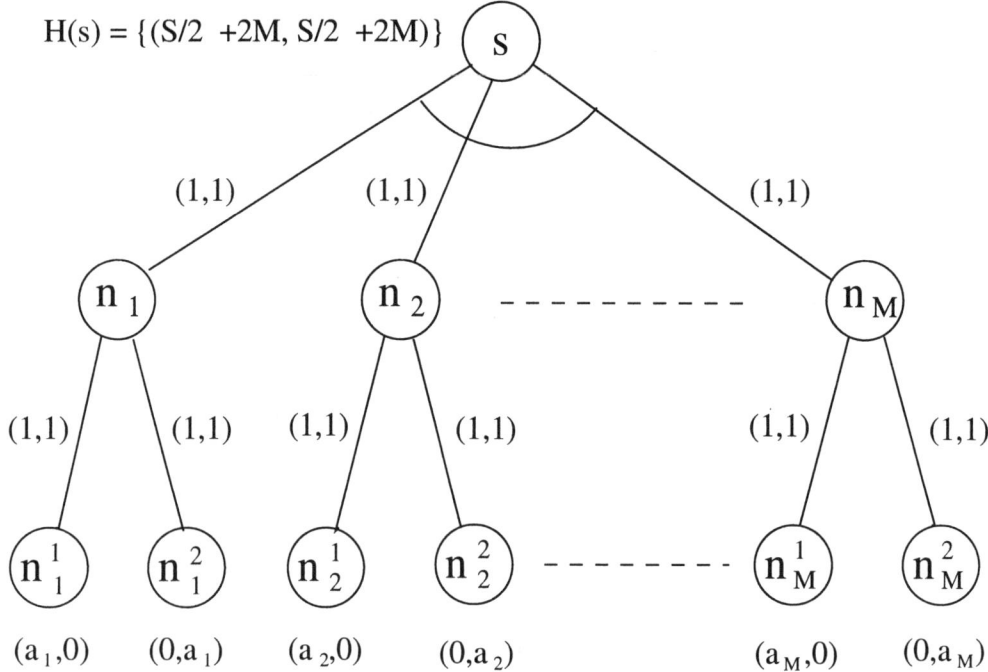

Figure 5.3: Selection using pathmax is NP-hard

$(a_i, 0)$ and node n_i^2 has a single cost vector $(0, a_i)$. The cost vector of each edge is $(1,1)$. The node s has a single heuristic vector:

$$h(s) = \left(\frac{S}{2} + 2M, \frac{S}{2} + 2M\right)$$

Given any partition P, the corresponding psg is identified by selecting the successor n_i^1 from every node n_i such that $i \in P$ and the successor n_i^2 from every node n_i such that $i \notin P$. It is easy to see that the psg corresponding to every valid partition will have a cost vector equal to $h(s)$. The cost vector of $psgs$ corresponding to partitions that are not valid will exceed $S/2 + 2M$ in either of the dimensions. If $pathmax$ is used then the cost vector of these $psgs$ will be dominated by $h(s)$. Thus the only $psgs$ that are non-dominated are those corresponding to valid partitions. This shows that the two-objective non-dominated psg identification problem is NP-hard. It is easy to see that the result follows for the general K-objective problem as well. □

5.4 Selection for monotone heuristics

In section 5.3 it was shown that if the heuristics are non-monotone, then the task of identifying a non-dominated cost psg is NP-hard. If the heuristics are monotone, then the question of $pathmax$ does not arise, and from the discussion in section 5.2 it follows

5.4 Selection for monotone heuristics

that using K-ordering at least one non-dominated *psg* can be identified in polynomial time.

It is easy to see that an admissible multiobjective scheme for this problem cannot terminate as long as the explicit AND/OR graph contains a *psg* having one or more non-dominated cost vectors. Until the first solution graph is found it is possible to identify (in each iteration) a non-dominated cost *psg* in polynomial time using an induced total order such as *K-order*. However, in the multiobjective framework search will typically continue (for other non-dominated solution graphs) after the first solution graph is obtained. Therefore in the general situation the explicit search space may contain some solution graphs and some other non-dominated *psgs*. We show that the task of identifying a non-dominated *psg* in such a general situation is NP-hard.

Theorem # 5.3 *Given an explicit additive AND/OR graph, the task of identifying a non-dominated* psg *is NP-hard in general.*
Proof: We show that any instance of the integer set partition problem can be reduced to the task of identifying a non-dominated *psg*. Given an instance of the integer set partition problem, we construct an AND/OR graph in the following way. The root node s is an OR-node with successors n_A, n_B and n_C (see Fig 5.4). n_B and n_C are terminal nodes with the following cost vectors:

$$C[n_B] = \left(\frac{S}{2} + 1 + 2M, 0\right) \quad \text{and} \quad C[n_C] = \left(0, \frac{S}{2} + 1 + 2M\right)$$

The cost vector of the solution graph $[s, n_B]$ is $(S/2 + 2 + 2M, 1)$ and that of the solution graph $[s, n_C]$ is $(1, S/2 + 2 + 2M)$.

The node n_A is an AND-node with successors $n_1, n_2, \ldots, n_M$ (there are M integers in A). Each n_i is an OR-node with two children n_i^1 and n_i^2. The node n_i^1 has a single cost vector $(a_i, 0)$ and node n_i^2 has the cost vector $(0, a_i)$. Given any partition P, the corresponding *psg* is identified by selecting n_A and the successor n_i^1 from every node n_i such that $i \in P$ and the successor n_i^2 from every node n_i such that $i \notin P$. It is easy to see that the *psg* corresponding to any valid partition will have a cost vector equal to $(S/2 + 1 + 2M, S/2 + 1 + 2M)$. The cost vectors of *psgs* corresponding to partitions that are not valid will exceed $S/2 + 1 + 2M$ in either of the dimensions, and will be dominated by the cost of either of the solution graphs $[s, n_B]$ and $[s, n_C]$.

Any admissible search scheme that finds the solution graphs $[s, n_B]$ and $[s, n_C]$ will still have to look for other non-dominated *psgs*. In Fig 5.4 the only other non-dominated cost *psgs* are those that correspond to valid partitions. Clearly the task of identifying any such *psg* is NP-hard.

This establishes that the general selection problem is NP-hard for the two-objective case. The result naturally follows for the general K-objective case. □

Theorem 5.3 shows that the complexity of the multiobjective problem differs from that of the conventional problem in the basic step of selection. In the following section we analyze the implications of this result and present a linear space search algorithm for this problem.

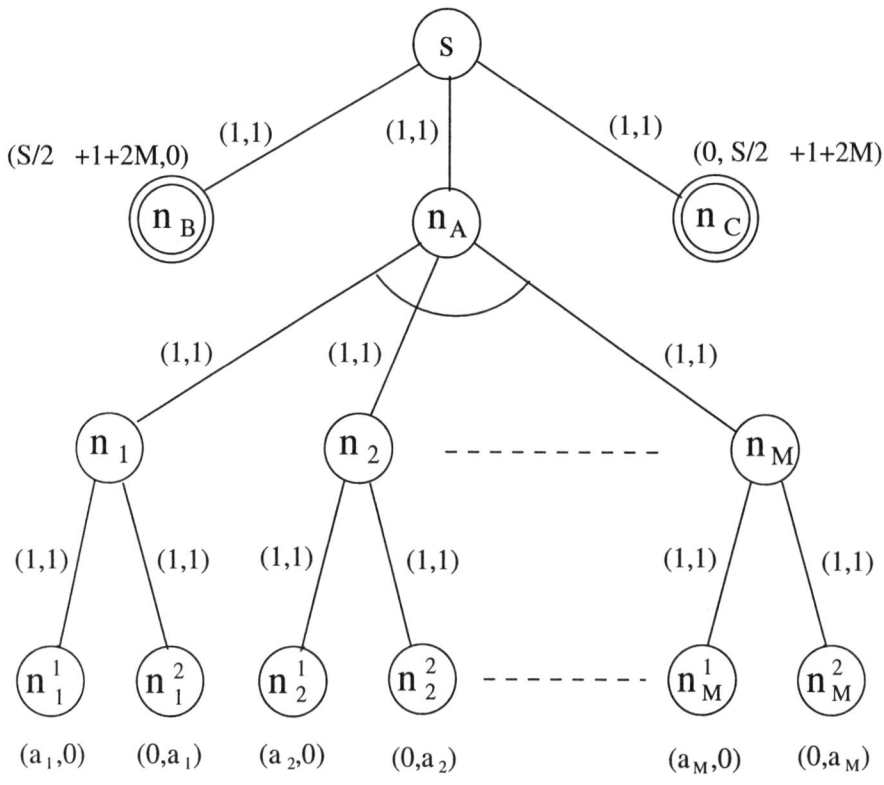

Figure 5.4: Graph illustrating that selection is NP-hard

5.5 The Algorithm: MObj*

The results presented in sections 5.3 and 5.4 have a direct bearing on the complexity of the AND/OR graph search problem. The major difference of the scenario depicted by these results from that of the conventional problem of single objective AND/OR graph search is on the following lines.

- Since the complexity of the task of identifying the minimum cost *psg* in an explicit single objective additive AND/OR graph is polynomial in the number of nodes in the graph, the complexity of AO^* is polynomial in the number of nodes it expands. Therefore the worst case complexity is polynomial in the number of nodes belonging to *psgs* whose cost is less than or equal to the optimal cost solution graph.

- The results presented in section 5.3 and section 5.4 show that in the multiobjective framework, the task of identifying a non-dominated cost *psg* in the explicit AND/OR graph is NP-hard in general. Thus, if S denotes the set of *maximal non-dominated psgs* (see definition 5.3) in the search-space graph, and Q denotes the

5.5 The Algorithm: MObj*

set of nodes belonging to the *psgs* in S, then it follows from the results presented in section 5.3 and section 5.4 that there cannot be a search strategy whose complexity is polynomial in the number of nodes in Q, (unless $P = NP$), even if the number of solutions is polynomial in Q.

In addition to this major difference, the complexity of cost revision in the multiobjective problem also differs from that of the conventional problem due to the following reason.

- In the multiobjective search framework, a tip node of the explicit graph can belong to multiple non-dominated *psgs* in the explicit graph. The number of non-dominated *psgs* that contain a common tip node can be exponential in the number of nodes in the explicit graph. When this tip node is expanded, the cost vectors of each of these *psgs* may change. To revise the cost vectors of each of these *psgs* we have to identify each of them, since only one of them can be marked at a given point of time. Since the general task of identifying non-dominated *psgs* is NP-hard, the cost revision step can be prohibitively expensive.

The above difficulties prompts us to adopt the following two policies.

1. Instead of revising the cost vectors of all *psgs* containing the node which is expanded, we revise the cost vectors of only those *psgs* that are generated from the currently selected *psg*.

2. Since the cost vectors of the other *psgs* are not being revised at the time of expansion of the node, we do not retain these *psgs* in the memory. This policy effectively implies that the search is performed using linear space.

The first policy implies that in the worst case, a node may be treated separately by every *psg* where it is a tip node. In the worst case, the same node may be expanded as many times as the number of distinct non-dominated *psgs* where it is a tip node. Taking this into consideration, the number of nodes which may be expanded in the worst case is given by:

$$T = \sum_{n \in Q} CARD(P(n)) \qquad (5.1)$$

where $P(n)$ denotes the set of *maximal non-dominated psgs* having n as a tip node and $CARD(P(n))$ denotes the number of *psgs* in the set $P(n)$. We now present a linear space search strategy $MObj^*$ that expands $O(T^2)$ nodes in the worst case (including node re-expansions).

5.5.1 General philosophy of $MObj^*$

The algorithm $MObj^*$ is a generalization of the algorithm $MOMA^*0$ presented in chapter 3. Search proceeds in a K-ordered best-first manner, that is, the *psg* with the mini-

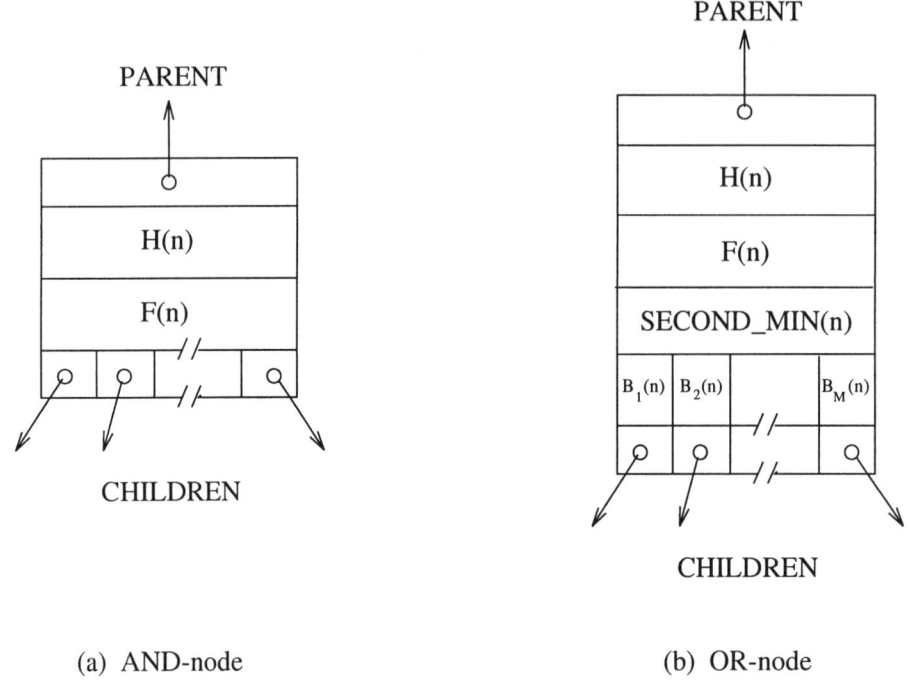

(a) AND-node   (b) OR-node

Figure 5.5: The structure of AND-nodes and OR-nodes

mum non-dominated cost in K-order is always selected first. This policy has been adopted considering the following two issues.

- It has been shown in section 5.2 that the use of an induced total order in essential in selecting non-dominated successors of OR-nodes.

- As shown in chapter 3, if the search proceeds in a K-ordered best-first manner then it is possible to back up a single cost vector while backtracking, and yet guarantee admissibility.

We describe the basic features of the algorithm in brief. In the following discussion when the terms *greater, less, minimum, maximum* etc. are used with respect to vectors, we mean that the comparison is on the basis of *K-order*.

The structure of AND-nodes and OR-nodes are shown in Fig 5.5. In a node n, $F(n)$ denotes the set of non-dominated cost vectors of *psgs* rooted at n (using *pathmax* if the heuristics are non-monotone). In an OR-node n, for every successor n_i of n, we have a cost $B_i(n)$ which denotes the minimum cost vector among all *psgs* where n_i is the successor of n.

The following are the characteristic features of algorithm $MObj^*$.

5.5 The Algorithm: MObj*

Use of GL: Algorithm MObj* uses a vector called GL (greatest lower bound), which holds the cost vector of the current *best psg*.

The representative cost vector of a psg: The minimum non-dominated cost vector among the set of cost vectors of a *psg* is called the representative cost vector of the *psg*.

Only the current psg is explicit: MObj* retains only the current *psg* in the memory. Whenever the algorithm backtracks to select some other *psg*, it prunes the nodes that do not belong to the new *psg*.

Use of SECOND_MIN(n): Whenever an OR-node n is expanded, the representative cost vector of each *psg* that is generated from the current *psg* by selecting different successors of the OR-node are computed. The *psg* with minimum representative cost vector is selected, and the cost vector of the next best *psg* is backed up at the node n in a vector called SECOND_MIN(n).

Use of NEXT_MIN: The minimum of the SECOND_MIN of all OR-nodes in the current *psg* is called NEXT_MIN. Thus NEXT_MIN denotes the cost vector of the next best *psg*. The algorithm backtracks when the representative cost vector of the current *psg* exceeds NEXT_MIN, and selects the *psg* having the cost vector NEXT_MIN.

Backtracking and cost back-up: In order to backtrack to the *psg* that had the cost vector NEXT_MIN, algorithm $MObj^*$ remembers the sequence in which the nodes of the current *psg* were expanded. It can backtrack to the *psg* of cost vector NEXT_MIN as follows.

> Let n be the node such that SECOND_MIN(n) is equal to NEXT_MIN. Also suppose that n is the ith node that was expanded in the current *psg*. Then the nodes that were generated after the expansion of n are pruned. The successor n_q of n, such that $B_q(n)$ is equal to SECOND_MIN(n), is selected next.

Let n_j be the previous successor of n. Then during backtracking, the minimum among the cost vectors of the current *psg* and the SECOND_MIN of all pruned OR-nodes is backed up at node n as $B_j(n)$.

Use of Minf: The function *Minf* is used for the same reason as has been done in algorithm $MOMA^*0$ (see chapter 3). Whenever the cost vector of any psg is evaluated, it must be updated to the *minimum vector which is greater than or equal to GL, but dominated by (or equal to) some heuristic vector of the psg*. This cost vector is assigned by the function *Minf*.

Test for dominance: If the representative cost vector of a *psg* is found to be dominated by the cost vector of some solution graph at the time of its selection, then the next best cost vector of the *psg* becomes the new representative cost vector. If all the cost vectors are dominated, then the cost vector of the psg is assigned infinity.

Note that if a solution graph is re-discovered then its cost vector will therefore be taken as infinity.

Since the search proceeds in K-order, it is easy to see that the first dimension of the representative cost vector of the selected *psg* is greater than or equal to the first dimension of the cost vector of every solution graph found so far. Therefore, while testing for dominance against the cost vector of a solution graph, we ignore the first dimension.

Termination condition: The algorithm terminates when the cost of every *psg* rooted at the source node s is computed as infinity.

5.5.2 Outline of MObj*

The outline of the algorithm is given below. The cost vectors of previous solution graphs are stored in a list called SOLUTION_COSTS. The function *min* returns the minimum cost vector (in K-order) from a set of cost vectors. The cost vectors of *psg*s are computed using the function *Minf* described in section 5.5.2.

Algorithm MObj*
1. [INITIALIZE]
   SOLUTION_COSTS $\leftarrow \phi$; NEXT_MIN $\leftarrow \infty$;
   Compute $H(s)$. Assign the minimum cost vector in K-order from $H(s)$ to GL.

2. [TERMINATE]
   If $GL = \infty$ THEN terminate.

3. [IDENTIFY SOLUTIONS]
   If all the tip nodes of the current psg are terminal nodes then
      3.1 Enter the cost vector of this solution graph in SOLUTION_COSTS
      3.2 Output the solution graph and Goto [Step 5]

4. [EXPAND]
   4.1 Select a non-terminal tip node n of the current psg.
   4.2 Expand node n to generate all its successors.
   4.3 If n is an AND-node, revise the cost of the psg and Goto [Step 4.5]
   4.4 If n is an OR-node:
      4.4.1 Revise the costs of each new-born psg and select the one that has
         the minimum representative cost vector.
      4.4.2 Assign SECOND_MIN(n) the representative vector of the next best psg.
      4.4.3 Set NEXT_MIN $\leftarrow$ min{NEXT_MIN,SECOND_MIN(n)}
   4.5 If the representative vector of the psg is less than or equal to NEXT_MIN then
      4.5.1 Assign this cost vector to GL and Goto [Step 2]
      Else Goto[Step 5]

5. [SELECT, PRUNE & ITERATE]
   5.1 Identify the psg corresponding to NEXT_MIN (call it NEXT_PSG)

5.5 The Algorithm: MObj*

  5.2 If NEXT_MIN is dominated by SOLUTION_COSTS then
    5.2.1 Revise the cost of NEXT_PSG.
    5.2.2 Set NEXT_MIN the minimum of SECOND_MIN of all OR-nodes.
    5.2.3 Goto [Step 5.1]
  5.3 Backtrack to NEXT_PSG
    5.3.1 Backup in $B_j(n)$ the minimum among the cost vectors of the previous psg and the SECOND_MIN of all OR-nodes in the previous psg where n is the OR-node up to which the algorithm backtracks and n_j was the successor of n in the previous psg.
    5.3.2 Instead of n_j select n_q where $B_q(n)$ = NEXT_MIN
  5.4 Set SECOND_MIN(n) $\leftarrow min\{B_i(n),\ i \neq q\}$
  5.5 Set NEXT_MIN the minimum of SECOND_MIN of all OR-nodes in new psg
  5.6 Set GL equal to the representative vector of the new psg and Goto [Step 2].

The function: *Minf*

Whenever the algorithm MObj* computes the representative cost vector of a *psg*, it updates the vector using the following function. The motivation for using this function is the same as in the case of the algorithm MOMA*0 presented in chapter 3. We shall illustrate its utility in the current context through an example.

  Minf(f, GL)
    f and GL are K-dimensional vectors.
    Let f_j denote the jth dimension of the cost vector f.
    Let L_j denote the jth dimension of GL.
    1. For $j = 1$ to $j = K$
        If $L_j \geq f_j$ then Set $f_j \leftarrow L_j$, else Goto [Step 2].
    2. Return f.

The following example explains the working of the algorithm *MObj** and the utility of the function *Minf*.

Example # 5.3 We show the operation of *MObj** on the graph of Fig 5.6. The set of heuristic vectors computed at each node is shown beside the node. We have considered a simple example where every node except node n_1 has a single heuristic vector.

The algorithm starts with the implicit specification of the AND/OR graph and the start node s. In the first iteration s is expanded to generate n_1 and n_2. The set of cost vectors of the *psg* comprising of the nodes $[s, n_1, n_2]$ is computed as $\{(6,5,6),(6,6,5)\}$.

In the second iteration n_1 is expanded. This gives birth to two new *psgs*, namely $[s, n_1, n_2, n_3]$ of cost $(8, 9, 9)$ and $[s, n_1, n_2, n_8]$ of cost $(9, 10, 10)$. The *psg* $[s, n_1, n_2, n_3]$ is selected. The vector $(9, 10, 10)$ is backed up as $B_2(n_1)$. The vector SECOND_MIN(n_1) also becomes $(9, 10, 10)$. Since there is no other OR-node in the explicit graph, the vector NEXT_MIN also becomes $(9, 10, 10)$. Node n_8 is pruned.

In the third iteration n_3 is expanded to generate two new *psgs*, namely $[s, n_1, n_2, n_3, n_4]$ of cost $(9, 10, 12)$ and $[s, n_1, n_2, n_3, n_5]$ of cost $(8, 11, 12)$. Since search proceeds in K-order, the *psg*

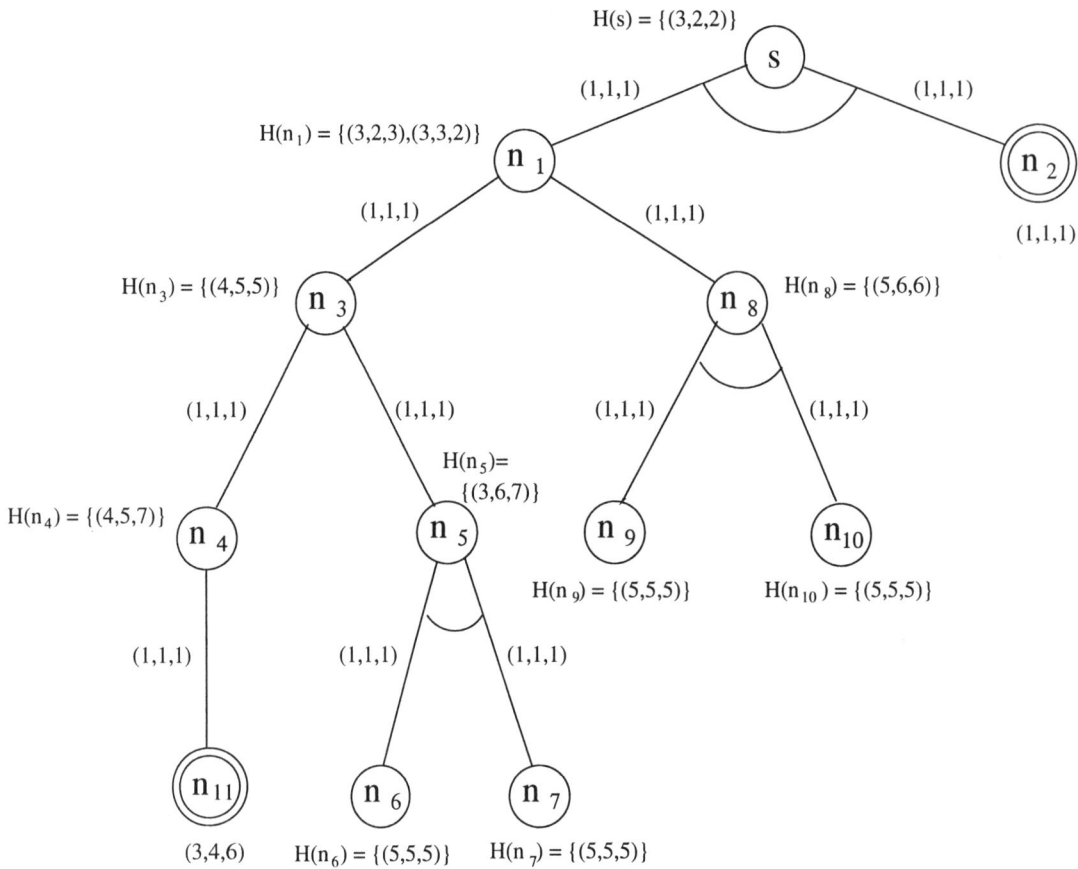

Figure 5.6: Graph illustrating the utility of *Minf*

$[s, n_1, n_2, n_3, n_5]$ is selected. The vector SECOND_MIN(n_3) (and $B_1(n_3)$) is set to $(9, 10, 12)$. The vector NEXT_MIN remains $(9, 10, 10)$. Node n_4 is pruned.

In the fourth iteration n_5 is expanded to generate the *psg* $[s, n_1, n_2, n_3, n_5, n_6, n_7]$ of cost $(17, 17, 17)$. This cost vector exceeds NEXT_MIN indicating that a better *psg* exists. Accordingly, $MObj^*$ backtracks to the *psg* $[s, n_1, n_2]$ and re-generates n_8. This backtracking is possible since $MObj^*$ remembers the order in which the nodes in the current *psg* is expanded. It knows that it has to backtrack up to the *psg* $[s, n_1, n_2]$ since SECOND_MIN(n_1) equals NEXT_MIN. It also knows that the second successor of n_1 (that is, n_8) has to be re-generated because $B_2(n_1)$ equals NEXT_MIN. After selecting the *psg* $[s, n_1, n_2, n_8]$, the nodes n_3, n_5, n_6 and n_7 are pruned.

While backtracking, $MObj^*$ backs up the minimum cost vector (in K-order) from the pruned space. In this case the best cost vector in the pruned space is $(9, 10, 12)$ that was backed up as SECOND_MIN(n_3). This vector is now backed up as $B_1(n_1)$. Consequently the vectors SECOND_MIN(n_1) and NEXT_MIN also become $(9, 10, 12)$.

5.5 The Algorithm: MObj*

In the fifth iteration n_8 is expanded to generate the *psg* $[s, n_1, n_2, n_8, n_9, n_{10}]$ of cost $(16, 16, 16)$. This cost vector exceeds NEXT_MIN. Therefore $MObj^*$ backtracks to the *psg* $[s, n_1, n_2]$ again and re-generates node n_3. Nodes n_8, n_9 and n_{10} are pruned. $B_2(n_1)$, SECOND_MIN(n_1) and NEXT_MIN are assigned the vector $(16, 16, 16)$.

In the sixth iteration n_3 is re-expanded to re-generate the *psgs* $[s, n_1, n_2, n_3, n_4]$ and $[s, n_1, n_2, n_3, n_5]$. If we do not use *Minf* then the cost vectors of these *psgs* will be $(9, 10, 12)$ and $(8, 11, 12)$ respectively. In that case $MObj^*$ will select $[s, n_1, n_2, n_3, n_5]$ and re-expand node n_5 to re-generate the *psg* of cost $(17, 17, 17)$. Then it will backtrack and select the *psg* $[s, n_1, n_2, n_3, n_4]$. We now show that by using *Minf*, we can avoid the re-expansion of n_5.

Since the backed up cost vector of the selected *psg* $[s, n_1, n_2, n_3]$ was $(9, 10, 12)$, it follows that no *psg* can have a cost vector less than $(9, 10, 12)$ in K-order. Again, the heuristic vector $(8, 11, 12)$ of the *psg* $[s, n_1, n_2, n_3, n_5]$ implies that the cost vector of every solution graph generated by extending the *psg* will be dominated by (or be equal to) $(8, 11, 12)$. The function *Minf* updates the cost vector of the *psg* to $(9, 11, 12)$. Note that the updated cost vectors can only be used to determine the order in which *psgs* are examined. Dominance testing is always done on the original cost vectors computed from the heuristic vectors of the tip nodes of the *psg*.

If we select on the basis of the cost vectors assigned by *Minf*, then the *psg* $[s, n_1, n_2, n_3, n_4]$ will be selected first. Consequently, node n_4 will be expanded to generate node n_{11}. This will yield the solution graph $[s, n_1, n_2, n_3, n_4, n_{11}]$ of cost $(9, 10, 12)$. Since search proceeds in K-order, it follows that by extending the *psg* $[s, n_1, n_2, n_3, n_5]$ of cost $(8, 11, 12)$ we cannot get any solution graph whose cost is non-dominated by $(9, 10, 12)$ (this is the reason for our ignoring the first dimension of the cost of a *psg* when testing for dominance by the cost of a solution graph). It is easy to see that the algorithm terminates without expanding any more nodes. □

5.5.3 Admissibility of MObj*

In this section, we establish the admissibility of $MObj^*$ under the following basic assumptions about the search space.

Assumption # 5.1 *The number of children of a node are finite.*

Assumption # 5.2 *All solution graphs are of finite size and have finite cost vectors, and the cost vectors of infinite psgs are dominated by solution graphs.*

Assumption # 5.3 *The heuristic function is admissible.*

Lemma # 5.1 *A node is expanded by $MObj^*$ only if it belongs to at least one non-dominated psg.*
Proof: By maintaining *pathmax* during cost revision, it is automatically ensured that the cost vector of a *psg* cannot decrease when it is expanded. The use of the function *Minf* to assign cost vectors to re-expanded *psgs* ensures that the cost vectors of a re-expanded *psg* is lowerbounded by the cost vector which was backed up during backtracking.

When MObj* selects a node for expansion, the selected *psg* is the one with minimum representative cost vector. If there were any *psg* with a lesser cost vector then the algorithm would have backtracked to the *psg* which had offered that cost vector. Since cost vectors of *psg*s can only increase (or remain same) due to expansion, no *psg* having a lesser cost vector (in K-order) can be found subsequently. Thus the *psg* selected by $MObj^*$ is always non-dominated. The result follows. □

Lemma 5.1, assumption 5.1 and assumption 5.2 prove that the set of nodes expanded by $MObj^*$ is finite. This does not guarantee termination, since the same set of nodes may be re-expanded indefinitely. The following lemma proves that such is not the case.

Lemma # 5.2 *In the worst case a psg is re-generated a finite number of times before a new node in some psg is expanded.*
Proof: $MObj^*$ backtracks from the current *psg* due to either of the following two reasons:

1. The representative cost vector of the *psg* exceeds NEXT_MIN.
2. The representative vector is dominated by some solution graph.

If all the cost vectors of a psg are dominated, then the cost of the *psg* becomes infinity and $MObj^*$ selects some other *psg*. If the same happens for all *psg*s then ∞ is backed up at every OR-node, and the algorithm terminates. Thus in the worst case a dominated *psg* can be re-generated a finite number of times before, either the algorithm terminates or a non-dominated *psg* is selected.

If a *psg* is selected for a second time then it is extended until the representative cost vector of the extended *psg* exceeds the previous backed up cost vector. If no new node is expanded, then the cost can only increase if its representative cost vector becomes dominated and a new representative vector is computed for the *psg*. Since the number of heuristic vectors at each node is finite and each time the *psg* is found dominated, at least one heuristic vector is deleted, the above case can occur only a finite number of times before either all cost vectors become dominated or a new node is expanded. Since a dominated *psg* may be re-generated only a finite number of times, the result follows. □

Theorem # 5.4 *Algorithm $MObj^*$ is admissible, that is, it terminates with all non-dominated solution graphs.*
Proof: The proof of termination follows directly from lemma 5.2, lemma 5.1, assumption 5.1 and assumption 5.2. If the number of nodes expanded is finite, and these nodes are expanded only a finite number of times, then the algorithm must terminate.

Let us assume that S_g is a non-dominated solution graph which is not found by $MObj^*$. Assuming that there is at least one OR-node in the graph (otherwise admissibility is obvious), it is easy to see that the first OR-node expanded by $MObj^*$ must belong to all solution graphs.

Let n be the first OR-node in the current *psg* (in the order of expansion) such that the child n_i of n in the current *psg* differs from the child n_j of n in S_g. If n_j has never been expanded, then $B_j(n)$ is the minimum cost vector (in K-order) of a subgraph of S_g and is therefore less

5.5 The Algorithm: MObj*

than or equal to the cost vector of S_g. Therefore, even if $MObj^*$ backtracks then the backed up cost vector must be less than or equal to $B_j(n)$ in K-order. This shows that if n_j has been re-generated then $B_j(n)$ must be less (in K-order) than the cost vector of S_g.

Therefore, until S_g is found at least one OR-node will have a backed up cost vector which is less than the cost vector of S_g. Since $MObj^*$ cannot terminate until all backed up costs are infinity, it follows that S_g must be found by $MObj^*$. □

We have assumed (assumption 5.3) that, for each solution graph $D(n)$ rooted at node n, there exists a heuristic in $H(n)$ which either dominates $C(D(n))$ or is equal to it. For heuristic functions where this cannot be assured, $MObj^*$ is not guaranteed to find all non-dominated solutions. For example, if there is a solution graph $D(n)$ rooted at node n, such that there is no under-estimate of $C(D(n))$ in $H(n)$, then $MObj^*$ is not guaranteed to find those non-dominated solution graphs which has $D(n)$ as a subgraph. It is easy to see that under such circumstances the following are true.

- $MObj^*$ finds all non-dominated solutions which do not contain any node where the above situation occurs.

- Brute force search appears to be necessary in order to guarantee admissibility of the search strategy.

To illustrate the second issue let us assume that there exists a solution graph $D(n)$ rooted at node n, such that there is no vector in $H(n)$ that dominates $C(D(n))$ or is equal to it. Now, if every cost vector of the *psgs* that has n as a tip node is dominated by the cost of solution graphs, then the *psg* will be considered dominated. If $D(n)$ is a subgraph of some non-dominated solution graph $D(s)$ then $D(s)$ will never be found by a strategy that considers only non-dominated *psgs*.

5.5.4 Complexity of MObj*

In this section we analyze the space and time complexities of $MObj^*$.

Theorem # 5.5 *The algorithm $MObj^*$ requires no more space than that occupied by the largest non-dominated* psg *in the entire search space.*
Proof: Follows from the fact that a *psg* is extended only if it has one or more non-dominated cost vectors and the fact that pruning occurs as soon as the algorithm backtracks. □

Theorem # 5.6 *The algorithm $MObj^*$ expands at most $O(T^2)$ nodes including re-expansions, where T is as defined in equation 5.1.*
Proof: The algorithm M_Obj^* expands a node only if it belongs to a non-dominated *psg*. Therefore, it can expand at most T new nodes according to our policy of treating nodes that are common to different *psgs* as separate nodes. Between expansion of new nodes $MObj^*$ may have to re-expand all previous nodes in the worst case. Thus, the total number of nodes expanded by $MObj^*$ in the worst case is $\sum_{i=1}^{T} i$, which is $O(T^2)$. □

5.5.5 MObj* for OR-graphs

In the absence of AND-nodes, it is easy to see that a *psg* is the same as a *path* from the source node to a single tip node of the explicit graph. Thus for every node n in the graph, we can have only one *psg* which has n as a tip node. Therefore, in equation 5.1 the value of $CARD(P(n))$ is always one. It follows that T is equal to the number of nodes in Q.

Thus for OR-graphs, $MObj^*$ expands $O(T^2)$ nodes in the worst case where T is the set of nodes belonging to non-dominated paths. This shows that $MObj^*$ is equivalent to $MOMA^*0$ in terms of number of node expansions. It is easy to see that the space complexity of the two algorithms is also identical since both of them require no more space than the size of the maximum non-dominated path in the search space.

5.6 Conclusion

In this chapter we have shown that the task of selection in best-first search of multiobjective additive AND/OR graphs is NP-hard in general. It may be interesting to note that the task of selection in a single objective AND/OR graph was also shown to be NP-hard [41]. However when additive costs are used only then polynomial time selection becomes possible [62, 63]. Our result establishes that in multiobjective AND/OR graphs, selection is NP-hard even if additive cost computation is used.

The chapter also points out that an induced total order (such as K-order) is essential for selection. The linear space algorithm MObj* uses this policy effectively. The steps leading to this algorithm were based on the arguments presented in this chapter. Other algorithms may be suggested by taking different approaches to the problem.

Chapter 6

Multiobjective Game Tree Search

The study of game playing situations and the task of developing intelligent game playing strategies has been one of the most popular topics in artificial intelligence. Besides popular games such as chess, checkers and GO, game playing situations also arise in many problems of practical significance where an adversary is present [75].

Most of the research on games have been around *two-player, perfect information* games. There are two adversary players who alternate in making moves, each viewing the opponent's failure as its own success. At each turn, the rules of the game define what moves are legal and what effect each possible move will have, leaving no room for chance. Therefore given any two states of the game, the common practice is to assume that the state which is considered better for a player on the basis of its evaluation function will be considered worse by its opponent. This is the basis for the MIN-MAX evaluation that is common to most game tree search strategies.

In many games of moderate complexity, comparison between two states of the game is based on multiple criteria, such as the various *tactical* and *positional* criteria considered in chess. It is generally accepted [4] that the task of combining these criteria into a single evaluation function is a matter of individual judgement and experience. Since the knowledge used in this task is normally not shared with the opponent, it is often inappropriate to assume that the state considered to be better by a player (on the basis of its own knowledge) will be considered worse by the opponent. Only in the specific cases where a state of the game is better than another in every criteria can a player be certain that the opponent will consider the former state to be worse than the latter.

Thus in such game playing situations, the information shared amongst the players is effectively a partial order on the states of the game. The decision making *strategies* of the individual players may be dictated by their own knowledge and judgement, but every rational strategy must be consistent with the partial order. This leads to an interesting variant of the game tree search problem (which we call the *multiobjective game tree search problem*) where each player knows its own *strategy* for comparing two states of the game but does not know the strategy of its opponent except on those cases where the partial order itself decides the better (or worse) of two states.

In the game playing situations considered so far, the sole objective of the game playing strategy is to win the game. It is only in the evaluation of a state of the game that multiple criteria are considered, leading to the situation where the information shared amongst the players is a partial order. Similar situations also arise in multi-criteria game playing, where the objective is not simply to win, but to reach a state of the game which is considered best on the basis of multiple non-commensurate criteria. It is easy to envisage such game playing situations in multi-criteria competitive optimization problems where the task is to perform multi-criteria optimization in the presence of an adversary. We elaborate through the following example.

Example # 6.1 Papadimitriou and Yannakakis [71] have described an extension of the *Traveling Salesperson Problem (TSP)* called the *Canadian TSP* where the salesperson has to optimize the cost of the tour in the presence of a malicious adversary who may put obstacles in any path, thereby increasing the cost of the path. It has been stated in [71] that the Canadian TSP can be conveniently modeled as a game playing problem. It is easy to see that if the salesperson has a dual objective of optimizing both the *cost* and the *time* required for the tour and the adversary puts obstacles which increases both the time and cost, then the Canadian TSP problem takes the form of a multi-criteria competitive optimization problem that may be modeled as a multi-criteria game playing situation. □

This chapter presents a scheme[1] for modeling and solving game tree search problems where the information shared amongst the players is a partial order. In the proposed framework it is assumed that the evaluation function returns a vector at each state of the game where each dimension of the *cost vector* of a state (also called an *outcome* in the present context) represents a distinct criterion under consideration. The objective of the search mechanism is to use the given partial order to prune the move sequences that lead to clearly inferior outcomes for a player and find the non-inferior options available to the player. The partial order on the vector valued outcomes is defined by the following relation.

Def # 6.1 Dominance:
Let $y^1 \equiv (y_1^1, y_2^1, \ldots, y_K^1)$ and $y^2 \equiv (y_1^2, y_2^2, \ldots, y_K^2)$ be two K-dimensional vectors. Then y^1 dominates y^2 iff:
$$y_i^1 \geq y_i^2 \quad \forall i, \ 1 \leq i \leq K \quad \text{and} \quad y^1 \neq y^2$$
A vector $y \in Y$ is said to be "non-dominated" in Y if there does not exist another vector $y' \in Y$ such that y' dominates y. □

---

[1]Reprinted from *Artificial Intelligence*, 82, Dasgupta, Chakrabarti, DeSarkar, *Searching Game Trees under a Partial Order*, 237-257, 1996, with permission from Elsevier Science.

6.1 The problem definition

It may be noted that the above definition of *dominance* is exactly the dual of the definition presented in chapter 2. The reason for this is that in the game playing problem the objective of a player is to *maximize* its benefits unlike in the minimization problems considered in the previous chapters.

This chapter analyzes the problem of searching game trees under the partial order imposed by the dominance relation. The major results presented are as follows.

- We have established the necessary and sufficient conditions for a *set* of of outcomes to be inferior to another set of outcomes.

- It has been shown that even though the individual *strategy* of a player is known it cannot be used for selection at the interior nodes of the game tree unless the *strategy* of the other player is also known.

- An algebra called *Dominance Algebra* has been constructed to describe the relation between the sets of outcomes backed up at a node. We show that the set of non-inferior options of a player can be represented as a minimal expression of the proposed algebra.

- We have identified the shallow and deep pruning conditions for multiobjective game trees. We present a partial order game tree search strategy which uses these pruning conditions on lines similar to the α-β pruning strategy [46].

The chapter is organized as follows. In section 6.1 we introduce the multiobjective game tree search problem through illustrative examples and give a formal definition of the search problem. *Dominance Algebra* and its implications is considered in section 6.2. Section 6.3 presents a bottom-up scheme to determine the options of a player at every node of the game tree. In section 6.4 we describe pruning conditions similar to α-β for the multiobjective problem. In the same section we also present a partial order search strategy on lines similar to α-β pruning.

6.1 The problem definition

In the conventional game tree search problem, the values at the tip nodes of the game tree are members of a totally ordered set. Given the MIN-MAX values of the children of a node, it is possible to determine the MIN-MAX value of the parent simply by using the total order to decide which value is the best [75]. Depth-first algorithms such as α-β pruning [46] and best-first algorithms like SSS^* [92] use this total order to determine the MIN-MAX value of the root node in an efficient manner.

In the multiobjective game tree search problem, we only have a partial order on the vector valued outcomes. In the cases where the partial order can determine the better outcome, the choice is obvious. For example in Fig 6.1 (a), it is obvious that player-1 at the MAX-node P will select the move to the outcome $(11,5)$ since $(11,5)$ dominates both

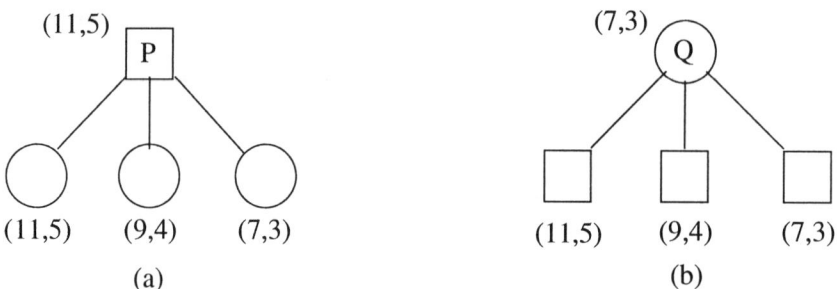

Figure 6.1: Simple cases of dominance

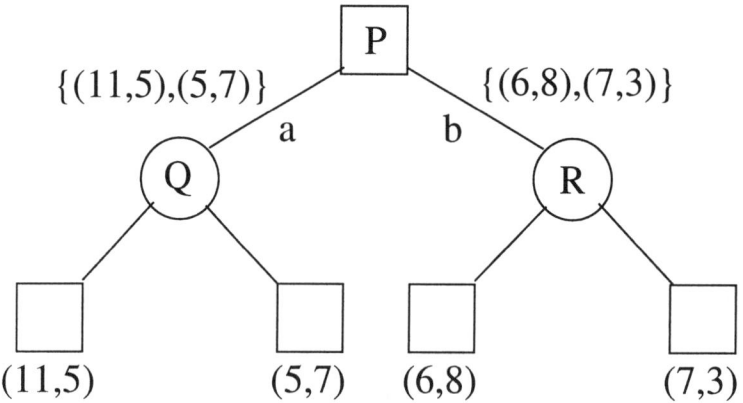

Figure 6.2: Case illustrating *sets* of outcomes

$(9,4)$ and $(7,3)$. Likewise, in Fig 6.1 (b) player-2 will select the move to the outcome $(7,3)$ from node Q. In such situations, it is possible to decide the best move without any knowledge of the individual judgement of the players. On the other hand, consider the situation in Fig 6.2. At node Q, player-2 has a choice between the outcomes $(11,5)$ and $(5,7)$. Since none dominates the other, the decision will be based on the judgement (or preferences) of player-2.

At node Q of Fig 6.2, if the preferences of player-2 is not known, then it is not possible for player-1 to decide which outcome will be selected. Therefore, corresponding to move a at node P, we have a set of possible outcomes $S_a = \{(11,5),(5,7)\}$. In a similar manner, corresponding to move b at node P, we have a set of outcomes $S_b = \{(6,8),(7,3)\}$. Thus, at node P, player-1 has to choose between the *sets of outcomes* S_a and S_b, and accordingly take either move a or move b. This choice will depend on the preferences of player-1. The question which arises at this point is: *how does a player use its preferences to choose between such sets of outcomes?*

Thus the problem of the player is to choose between two sets of vector valued outcomes (such as S_a and S_b) with the knowledge that the preferences of the opponent (which is

6.1 The problem definition

not known to this player) will decide the final outcome from the selected set. Let $\vec{x}$ denote the worst outcome in a given set based on the preferences of the player. Then the best that the given set can *guarantee* for the player is $\vec{x}$. This is similar to the familiar notion of MIN in conventional game tree search. Therefore, to compare two sets of outcomes based on individual preferences, we compare the worst outcome from each set based on those preferences. In case of a tie, we compare the other outcomes. The complete procedure is as follows:

Compare(S_1, S_2, ϕ)
To compare sets of outcomes S_1 and S_2 on the basis of preferences ϕ
1. If only S_1 is empty, then declare S_2 as better.
   Likewise, if only S_2 is empty, then declare S_1 as better.
   If both S_1 and S_2 are empty then select S_1 or S_2
   randomly and declare it to be better.
2. Let $\vec{x}_1$ be the worst outcome in S_1 and
   $\vec{x}_2$ be the worst outcome in S_2 based on ϕ.
3. If $\vec{x}_1$ and $\vec{x}_2$ are of equal preference then
   3.1 Drop all outcomes from S_1 and S_2 that are of
       equal preference to $\vec{x}_1$
   3.2 Goto [Step 1]
4. If $\vec{x}_1$ is better than $\vec{x}_2$ based on ϕ, then declare S_1 as better
   else declare S_2 as better.

As an example, if the preferences of player-1 is such that $(5, 7)$ is preferred over $(11, 5)$ and $(11, 5)$ is preferred over $(13, 3)$, then the set $\{(13, 3), (5, 7)\}$ is preferred over the set $\{(13, 3), (11, 5)\}$. Also the set $\{(13, 3), (5, 7)\}$ is preferred over the set $\{(13, 3)\}$, since depending on the preferences of the opponent there is a possibility of reaching the better outcome $(5, 7)$ from the former set.

It should also be noted that two outcomes may have equal preference. Thus, the preferences of a player is not exactly an induced total order on the set of vector valued outcomes; rather, it can be viewed as a many-to-one mapping from the set of outcomes to a totally ordered set which preserves the partial order imposed by the dominance relation. Throughout this chapter we assume that the players use the procedure *Compare* to compare the sets of outcomes. We define the strategy of a player as follows.

Def # 6.2 [A Strategy]:
The strategy of a player is a selection mechanism based on the procedure "Compare" and the individual preferences of the player which is consistent with the partial order imposed by the dominance relation. Thus if $\vec{x}$ is an outcome which dominates an outcome $\vec{y}$, then for all strategies of player-1, $\vec{x}$ is better than $\vec{y}$ and for all strategies of player-2, $\vec{y}$ is better than $\vec{x}$. □

It is easy to see that if the individual strategies of both players are known, then by applying the strategy of player-1 at MAX-nodes and the strategy of its opponent (player-2) at the MIN-nodes, we can solve the problem using conventional game tree search

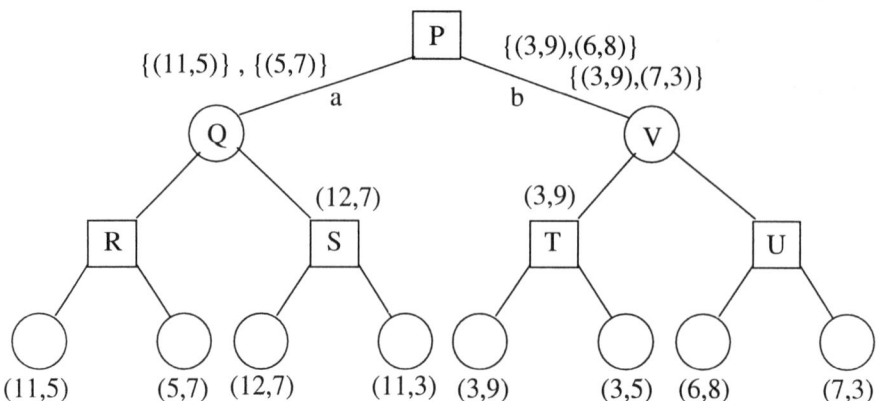

Figure 6.3: Case illustrating multiple sets of outcomes per move

schemes. However, the partial order game tree search problem is motivated from the natural assumption that a player does not know the strategy of its opponent. Initially we analyze the situation where the strategy of neither player is known to the search scheme. Later we shall show that even if the strategy of one player is known, it should not be used for selection in the interior nodes of the game tree.

In Fig 6.2, corresponding to each move at node P we had only one set of outcomes. The following example illustrates that corresponding to a move, it is possible to have multiple sets of outcomes.

Example # 6.2 Consider the game tree in Fig 6.3. At node T player-1 will obviously select the outcome $\{(3,9)\}$. At node U player-1 can choose either $(6,8)$ or $(7,3)$ depending on its strategy. Since this strategy is not known to player-2, then at node V, it has to choose between the sets $\{(6,8),(7,3)\}$ and $\{(3,9)\}$. Player-2 may choose either set depending on its own strategy. Now suppose the strategy of player-1 is such, that it prefers $(6,8)$ over $(7,3)$. If the game reaches node U, then it will select $(6,8)$. Therefore, corresponding to this strategy of player-1, move b (at node P) presents the set of outcomes $\{(3,9),(6,8)\}$ such that the opponent's strategy decides whether $(3,9)$ or $(6,8)$ will be reached. On the other hand, if player-1 prefers $(7,3)$ over $(6,8)$, then corresponding to that strategy, move b presents the set of outcomes $\{(3,9),(7,3)\}$. Thus, if move b is selected at node P, then the outcome will either belong to the set $\{(3,9),(6,8)\}$ or the set $\{(3,9),(7,3)\}$ depending on the strategy adopted by player-1.

In a similar situation at node Q, player-2 has to choose between the sets $\{(11,5),(5,7)\}$ and $\{(12,7)\}$. In this case, since both $(11,5)$ and $(5,7)$ are dominated by $(12,7)$, player-2 will always select the move to node R. Therefore, corresponding to move a, we have two singleton sets, namely $\{(11,5)\}$ and $\{(5,7)\}$.

At node P of Fig 6.3, we can provide player-1 with four sets of outcomes to choose from, namely $\{(11,5)\}$, $\{(5,7)\}$, $\{(3,9),(6,8)\}$ and $\{(3,9),(7,3)\}$. Are all these sets candidates for selection? Let us compare the sets $\{(11,5)\}$ and $\{(3,9),(7,3)\}$. Since $(11,5)$ dominates $(7,3)$, therefore it is easy to see (through the procedure *Compare*) that there can be no strategy for

6.1 The problem definition

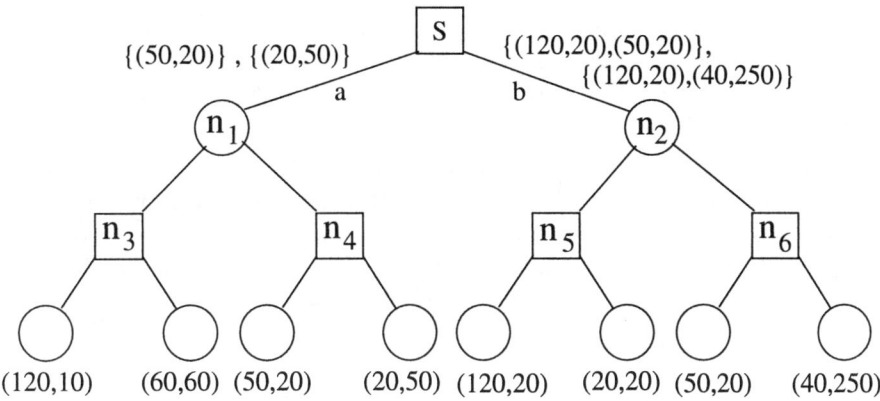

Figure 6.4: Case illustrating that preferences cannot be used in interior nodes

player-1 that prefers the set $\{(3,9),(7,3)\}$. This set is therefore an inferior set of outcomes. □

Example 6.2 shows that even if the individual strategies of the players are not known, certain sets of outcomes can be clearly discarded. The objective of partial order game tree search is to discard such sets of outcomes and provide the player at the root node with the non-inferior sets of outcomes.

Before giving the formal definition of the problem, it is necessary to make one further observation. Supposing that each player knows its own strategy but not that of its opponent. In the game tree representation, this means that only the strategy of player-1 is known. Can we use the strategy at the interior MAX-nodes of the game tree to prune away several sets of outcomes? The following example shows that the answer is negative in general.

Example # 6.3 Consider the game tree in Fig 6.4. Let the strategy of player-1 be such that given any two outcomes, the outcome which is greater in the first dimension is preferred. If two outcomes are equal in the first dimension, then the outcome with the larger second dimension is preferred. Let us first analyze the problem using the strategy of player-1 at the interior nodes. At node n_3 player-1 will choose the outcome $(120, 10)$, and at node n_4 it will select $(50, 20)$ based on its strategy. At node n_1, it is not known whether player-2 will select $(120, 10)$ or $(50, 20)$, and so corresponding to move a at node P, we have the set of outcomes $\{(120, 10), (50, 20)\}$. Likewise, player-1 will select $(120, 20)$ at node n_5 and $(50, 20)$ at node n_6. At node n_2, player-2 will definitely select $(50, 20)$ since it is dominated by $(120, 20)$. Thus corresponding to move b we have the set $\{(50, 20)\}$. If we compare the sets corresponding to move a and b on the basis of the strategy of player-1, we find that the set $\{(120, 10), (50, 20)\}$ is preferred over the set $\{(50, 20)\}$, and so, move a appears to be better.

In this analysis, we have overlooked one vital point, that is, the opponent does not know the strategy of player-1. Therefore, from the point of view of player-2, player-1 can select either of the outcomes at nodes n_3 and n_4. Therefore, at node n_1, player-2 has to choose between the sets $\{(120, 10), (60, 60)\}$ and $\{(50, 20), (20, 50)\}$. Since both $(50, 20)$ and $(20, 50)$

are better than $(60, 60)$ for every strategy of player-2, therefore player-2 will always select the set $\{(50, 20), (20, 50)\}$ and take the move to node n_4. Thus, corresponding to move a, we have two sets of outcomes, namely $\{(50, 20)\}$ and $\{(20, 50)\}$. For the given strategy of player-1, the set $\{(50, 20)\}$ is preferred.

Using a similar reasoning, at node n_2, player-2 will have to select between the sets $\{(120, 20)\}$ and $\{(50, 20), (40, 250)\}$. Since player-2 can select either set depending on its strategy, therefore corresponding to move b, we have two sets of outcomes, namely $\{(120, 20), (50, 20)\}$ and $\{(120, 20), (40, 250)\}$. For the given strategy of player-1, the set $\{(120, 20), (50, 20)\}$ is preferred. By comparing this set with the set $\{(50, 20)\}$ (which was preferred through move a) we find that actually move b is better for player-1. $\square$

The above example shows that unless the strategies of both players are known, we cannot apply the individual strategy of either player at an internal node while determining the sets of outcomes. Therefore, we can eliminate only those sets of outcomes that are inferior with respect to every strategy. In other words, we have to find the non-inferior *packets* of outcomes, where a *packet* of outcomes is defined as follows.

Def # 6.3 [Packet of outcomes]:
A set of outcomes P corresponding to a move "a" at a node n will be called a "packet" for a player iff it has the following two properties:

1. *There exists a strategy of the player, such that after taking move "a", irrespective of the strategy adopted by the opponent, the final outcome will be better than or equal to an outcome in that set in every dimension.*

2. *For every outcome $\vec{x}$ in P, there exists an opponent strategy such that if move "a" is taken, then the final outcome is $\vec{x}$.*

From the previous discussion it follows that there may be several packets corresponding to a single move. The set of packets at a node is the union of the set of packets corresponding to every move at that node. $\square$

The second property of a *packet* ensures that redundant outcomes (that is, outcomes which will never be reached) are not included in a *packet*. For example in Fig 6.4, the set of outcomes $\{(120, 10), (50, 20)\}$ corresponding to move a at node s satisfies the first property, but is not a packet for player-1 since the opponent at node n_1 will always select the move to n_4 (see example 6.3), and therefore there is no opponent strategy to reach the outcome $(120, 10)$.

If we can find the entire set of packets at the root node of the game tree, then what we have is the sets of outcomes corresponding to every strategy of the player at the root node. Out of the entire set of packets, some packets may be inferior to other packets for every strategy of the player. What are the necessary and sufficient conditions for a packet to be inferior among the set of packets at a node? We identify two conditions as follows.

6.1 The problem definition

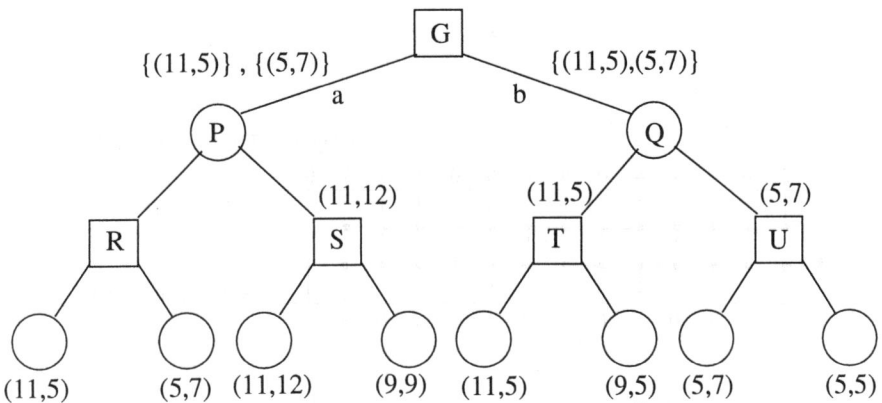

Figure 6.5: Dominance by freedom of choice

1. **Clear Dominance:** A packet P is inferior to a packet P' for a player if:

    1. Each outcome in P' is either equal or is strictly better than some outcome in P, and
    2. There exists at least one outcome in P' which is strictly better than some outcome in P.

    In such cases we say that P' dominates P by *clear dominance*.

2. **Dominance by Freedom of Choice:** A packet P is inferior to a set of packets $P_1, \ldots, P_J$ if each packet P_i contains fewer outcomes than in P, and the union of them yields P. In such cases we say that $P_1, \ldots, P_J$ dominates P by *freedom of choice*.

Before proving that these are the necessary and sufficient conditions for a packet to be inferior, we illustrate the idea of *dominance by freedom of choice* through an example. Note that the idea of *clear dominance* has already been illustrated in example 6.2 and example 6.3.

Example # 6.4 Consider the game tree in Fig 6.5. At node P, player-2 will always select the set $\{(11,5),(5,7)\}$ from the two sets $\{(11,5),(5,7)\}$ and $\{(11,12)\}$. Thus corresponding to move a at node G, we have two sets of outcomes, namely $\{(11,5)\}$ and $\{(5,7)\}$. At the nodes T and U, player-1 will always select $(11,5)$ and $(5,7)$ respectively. Thus, at node Q, player-2 can either select $(11,5)$ or $(5,7)$ depending on its strategy. Therefore, corresponding to move b we have the set of outcomes $\{(11,5),(5,7)\}$.

If the strategy of player-1 is such that $(11,5)$ is preferred over $(5,7)$, then the set $\{(11,5)\}$ will be preferred over $\{(11,5),(5,7)\}$ based on the procedure *Compare*. On the other hand, if the strategy of player-1 is such that $(5,7)$ is preferred over $(11,5)$, then $\{(5,7)\}$ will be preferred over $\{(11,5),(5,7)\}$. Thus, whatever be the strategy of player-1, the set $\{(11,5),(5,7)\}$ will never be selected. The sets $\{(11,5)\}$ and $\{(5,7)\}$ together provide more freedom of choice than the union $\{(11,5),(5,7)\}$ and therefore dominate the set $\{(11,5),(5,7)\}$. □

Theorem # 6.1 *The conditions of "clear dominance" and "dominance by freedom of choice" are sufficient conditions for a packet to be inferior among a set of packets.*
Proof: Suppose a packet P' dominates a packet P by *clear dominance*. Consider a strategy ST of the player. Let $\vec{x}$ be the worst outcome in P' based on ST. From the definition of clear dominance, there exists some outcome $\vec{y}$ in P which is either equal to $\vec{x}$ or worse for every strategy. If $\vec{y}$ is worse than $\vec{x}$ then P is obviously inferior. If $\vec{x}$ is equal to $\vec{y}$, we drop them from P and P', and use the same reasoning on the next worst outcome. Since there exists at least one outcome in P' which is strictly better than an outcome in P, it follows that P is inferior to P' for every strategy ST.

Suppose the set of packets $P_1, \ldots, P_J$ dominates a packet P by *freedom of choice*. Consider a strategy ST of the player. Let $\vec{x}$ be the best outcome in P on the basis of ST. From the definition of dominance by freedom of choice, there exists a packet P_i which is a subset of P and contains $\vec{x}$. Let us compare P_i and P on the basis of ST. If the worst outcome in P does not belong to P_i, then P is inferior. Otherwise, we drop that outcome from both sets and consider the next worst outcome and so on. Since P_i contains the best outcome in P and contains fewer outcomes than in P, therefore P is inferior to P_i for the strategy ST. It follows that P is inferior to at least one of the of packets $P_1, \ldots, P_J$ for every strategy. □

Theorem # 6.2 *For a packet to be inferior among a set of packets S, either "clear dominance" or "dominance by freedom of choice" necessarily hold.*
Proof: Let us consider a packet P which is neither dominated by *clear dominance*, nor by *freedom of choice*. Let P_u denote the union of all packets in S which are subsets of P. Let P' denote the set of outcomes in P that are not in P_u. Since P is not dominated by freedom of choice, therefore P' is non-empty. We now consider a strategy as follows:

1. Every outcome in P_u has equal priority. Every outcome in P' has equal priority. Outcomes from P' are preferred over outcomes from P_u.

2. Every outcome that does not dominate an outcome in P, or is not equal to an outcome in P, has a lower priority than every outcome in P.

Since P' is non-empty and its outcomes are preferred over those in P_u, it follows that P is preferred over all packets which are subsets of P. Since P is not dominated by "clear dominance", therefore every packet that is not a subset of P must contain an outcome which neither dominates nor is equal to an outcome in P. Therefore, P is preferred over such packets as well. It follows that P is the most preferred packet based on the above strategy, and therefore not an inferior packet. □

The game tree search problem studied in this chapter may now be defined as follows.

The Partial Order Game Tree Search Problem

Given: A game tree where the values at the tip nodes are K-dimensional vectors.

To find: The set of non-inferior packets at the root node of the game tree.

To address the above problem, we will first analyze the problem of finding the minimal set of packets at a node n when the set of packets for the player at node n are given. For this purpose we shall use an algebra called *Dominance Algebra*. Subsequently, we shall address the problem of determining the set of packets at a node using partial order game tree search.

6.2 Dominance Algebra

Given the set of packets at a node, we have to identify the set of non-inferior packets (that is, those that may be selected by the player at that node). For convenience of representation we use an algebra to describe the type of operations that take place at the MAX and MIN nodes.

At a given node n, we have a set of packets $P_1 \ldots P_m$ for the player who makes the move at that node. If n is a MAX-node, then we denote the options of player-1 at node n by a *MAX-expression* F_n as follows:

$$F_n = P_1 +_{max} P_2 +_{max} \cdots +_{max} P_m$$

The operator $+_{max}$ is a commutative operator. Following the definition of packet dominance, we define another property of the $+_{max}$ operator through the following *MAX-absorption law*.

MAX-absorption Law: A packet P_i at a MAX-node n can be absorbed under the following two situations:

Clear Dominance: There exists a packet P_j at node n such that each outcome in P_j dominates (or is equal to) some outcome in P_i, and at least one outcome in P_j dominates an outcome in P_i. If this condition holds then:

$$P_j +_{max} P_i = P_j$$

In other words, P_i is absorbed in the MAX-expression F_n at node n.

Dominance by Freedom of Choice: There exists a set of packets $P'_1 \ldots P'_J$ at node n such that each of them contains fewer outcomes than in P_i, and the union of them yields P_i. If this condition holds then:

$$(P'_1 +_{max} \cdots +_{max} P'_J) +_{max} P_i = P'_1 +_{max} \cdots +_{max} P'_J$$

In other words, P_i is absorbed in the MAX-expression F_n at node n.

Thus the $+_{max}$ operator is actually the dominance operator over packets of outcomes. Using MAX-absorption Law, we can obtain a minimal MAX-expression at node n. A MAX-expression is actually a *set* of packets over which we can apply MAX-absorption law to eliminate dominated packets. Therefore, throughout this chapter we may use statements such as " *a packet belongs to a MAX-expression*" or "*a packet is in a MAX-expression*".

We now prove that given the set of packets at node n, application of MAX-absorption Law leads to an unique minimal MAX-expression F_n for that node. The following lemma shows that the sequence in which dominated packets are absorbed does not affect the final MAX-expression.

Lemma # 6.1 *If F is a MAX-expression and P_1 and P_2 are packets such that $F +_{max} P_1 +_{max} P_2 = F$ (through some sequence of application of MAX-absorption law) then $F +_{max} P_1 = F$ and $F +_{max} P_2 = F$.*
Proof: It is easy to see that if $F +_{max} P_1 \neq F$, as well as $F +_{max} P_2 \neq F$, then $F +_{max} P_1 +_{max} P_2$ cannot be equal to F. Without loss of generality, let $F +_{max} P_1 = F$. (There is no loss of generality because $+_{max}$ is commutative). Now, if P_1 is not instrumental in the absorption of P_2, then the result follows trivially. Let us consider the cases where P_1 is used in the absorption of P_2. If P_1 is used in the absorption of P_2, then each outcome in P_1 must either dominate or be equal to some outcome in P_2.

The MAX-expression F can absorb P_1 through *clear dominance* or through *freedom of choice*. We analyze both situations:

Clear Dominance: If F absorbs P_1 through clear dominance, then there exists a packet P_i in the MAX-expression F, such that P_i clearly dominates P_1. Then each outcome in P_i either dominates or is equal to some outcome in P_1, and at least one outcome in P_i dominates an outcome in P_1. Since each outcome in P_1 in turn either dominates or is equal to some outcome in P_2, therefore P_i absorbs P_2 through clear dominance.

Dominance by Freedom of Choice: If F absorbs P_1 through freedom of choice then we can have two cases:

1. If P_1 absorbs P_2 through clear dominance, then there exists an outcome $\vec{x}$ in P_1 that dominates an outcome in P_2. Each outcome in P_1 must belong to some packet P_i in the MAX-expression F (from the definition of absorption by freedom of choice). Let P_i be the packet containing $\vec{x}$. Since every outcome in P_i is equal to some outcome in P_1, therefore P_i absorbs P_2 through clear dominance.

2. Since F absorbs P_1 through freedom of choice, therefore there exists packets $P'_1, \ldots, P'_J$ in the MAX-expression F, such that the set of packets $S_1 = \{P'_1, \ldots, P'_J\}$ dominates P_1 by freedom of choice. Now if P_1 is used to absorb P_2 by freedom of choice then there exists a set S_2 of packets in the MAX-expression F, such that $S_2 \cup \{P_1\}$ absorbs P_2. It is easy to see then that $S_2 \cup S_1$ can absorb P_2 by freedom of choice. Therefore F absorbs P_2 by freedom of choice.

□

The lemma effectively states that if P_1 is instrumental in the absorption of P_2, and P_1 is absorbed by F before the absorption of P_2 then F will also absorb P_2.

Theorem # 6.3 *Given the set of packets for player-1 at a MAX-node n, application of MAX-absorption Law leads to an unique minimal MAX-expression for node n.*
Proof: If a packet is instrumental in the absorption of another packet then lemma 6.1 shows that even if the former packet is absorbed earlier, the latter packet will still be absorbed. Thus

the absorption of the dominated packets is independent of the sequence in which the packets are absorbed. The result follows. □

Given the set of packets for player-1 at a MAX-node we can individually test each packet to see whether it is absorbed by the other packets. Theorem 6.3 shows that this will lead to an unique minimal set of packets at the node. It may be easily shown that a similar analysis may be applied to the packets for player-2 (the opponent) at a MIN-node. If n is a MIN-node, then we denote the options of player-2 at node n by a *MIN-expression* F_n as follows:

$$F_n = P_1 +_{min} P_2 +_{min} \cdots +_{min} P_m$$

$P_1, \ldots, P_m$ are packets for player-2 at node n. The operator $+_{min}$ is a commutative operator similar to $+_{max}$ except that it obeys the following *MIN-absorption law*.

MIN-absorption Law: A packet P_i at a MIN-node n can be absorbed under the following two situations:

Clear Dominance: There exists a packet P_j at node n such that each outcome in P_j is dominated by (or is equal to) some outcome in P_i, and at least one outcome in P_j is dominated by an outcome in P_i. If this condition holds then:

$$P_j +_{min} P_i = P_j$$

Dominance by Freedom of Choice: There exists a set of packets $P'_1 \ldots P'_J$ at node n such that each of them contains fewer outcomes than in P_i, and the union of them yields P_i. If this condition holds then:

$$(P'_1 +_{min} \cdots +_{min} P'_J) +_{min} P_i = P'_1 +_{min} \cdots +_{min} P'_J$$

Theorem # 6.4 *Given the set of packets for player-2 at a MIN-node n, application of MIN-absorption Law leads to an unique minimal MIN-expression for node n.*
Proof: On similar lines to the proof of theorem 6.3. □

Theorem 6.3 and theorem 6.4 effectively prove that the $+_{max}$ and $+_{min}$ operators are associative. Dominance algebra consists of sets (packets) of K-dimensional vectors and the two commutative and associative operators $+_{max}$ and $+_{min}$. Given the MAX-expression at a MAX-node (or a MIN-expression at a MIN-node), we can use the MAX-absorption law (MIN-absorption law) to obtain the minimal MAX-expression (MIN-expression) at that node.

6.3 Finding the packets

It is now known how to determine the minimal set of packets at a node when the entire set of packets at that node are given. Let us now address the problem of identifying the set of packets at a node. In particular, we address the following problems:

1. How to find the minimal set of packets for player-1 at a given MAX-node n when the minimal set of packets for player-2 at the child MIN-nodes are given.

2. How to find the minimal set of packets for player-2 at a given MIN-node n when the minimal set of packets for player-1 at the child MAX-nodes are given.

For the first problem, we define a function called *MIN-to-MAX* that converts a given MIN-expression to a MAX-expression. The function is based on the following result.

Lemma # 6.2 *Let $P_1, \ldots, P_m$ be the minimal set of packets for player-2 at a MIN-node n. If we construct a set S of outcomes by selecting one outcome from each P_i, $1 \leq i \leq m$, then S is a packet for the parent MAX-node of n.*
Proof: We show that there exists a strategy for player-1 such that the final outcome either dominates or is equal to some outcome in S. If player-2 does not make a mistake, then it will select one of the packets $P_1, \ldots, P_m$. Without loss of generality, let us assume that player-2 selects the packet P_i. Then from the definition of a packet there exists a strategy for player-1 to reach any desired outcome from P_i. The result follows because, by the construction of S, one outcome in P_i belongs to S.

If player-2 makes a mistake, then it will select a packet P' that can be absorbed by $P_1 +_{min} \cdots +_{min} P_m$. Then, *every* outcome in those packets that are instrumental in the absorption of P' will be either dominated by or equal to some outcome in P'. Thus, if player-2 selects P', then there exists a strategy for player-1 to reach an outcome from P' which is either better than some outcome in S or equal to it. It follows that S is a packet for player-1. □

The MIN-to-MAX function is as follows.

Function MIN-to-MAX(F: MIN-expression)
1. Let $F = P_1 +_{min} P_2 +_{min} \cdots +_{min} P_m$
2. Construct all possible sets of outcomes by selecting one outcome from each packet P_i, $1 \leq i \leq m$. Let these sets be $S_1, S_2, \ldots S_J$.
3. Using MAX-absorption Law, minimize the MAX-expression:
$F' = S_1 +_{max} S_2 +_{max} \cdots +_{max} S_J$
4. Return the MAX-expression F'.

Lemma # 6.3 *If n_i is the ith child of the MAX-node n and F_{n_i} is the MIN-expression corresponding to the MIN-node n_i, then the set of packets for player-1 at node n through the child n_i can be represented by the MAX-expression returned by MIN-to-MAX(F_{n_i}).*
Proof: From lemma 6.2 it follows that the set of packets constructed by the function MIN-to-MAX are packets for player-1 at node n. Once the game reaches node n_i, there exists a strategy for player-2 to ensure that the game reaches either some outcome from the selected packet at node n_i, or an outcome that is dominated by some outcome from the selected packet. Therefore, through node n_i player-1 can (at best) reach only those outcomes that are present in the packets at node n_i. The result follows. □

6.3 Finding the packets

Theorem # 6.5 *If F_{n_i} denotes the MIN-expression of the ith child of the MAX-node n, then the MAX-expression of the node n is:*
$$F_n = \text{MIN-to-MAX}(F_{n_1}) +_{max} \text{MIN-to-MAX}(F_{n_2}) +_{max} \cdots +_{max} \text{MIN-to-MAX}(F_{n_m})$$
where m denotes the number of children of node n.
Proof: Follows from lemma 6.3. □

The above analysis shows that using the MIN-to-MAX function, we can construct the set of packets (for player-1) at a MAX-node when the set of packets (for player-2) is given for each child MIN-node. The set of packets at a MIN-node can be constructed in a very similar fashion using the following MAX-to-MIN function.

Function MAX-to-MIN(F: MAX-expression)
1. Let $F = P_1 +_{max} P_2 +_{max} \cdots +_{max} P_m$
2. Construct all possible sets of outcomes by selecting one outcome from each packet P_i, $1 \leq i \leq m$. Let these sets be $S_1, S_2, \ldots S_J$.
3. Using MIN-absorption Law, minimize the MIN-expression:
$$F' = S_1 +_{min} S_2 +_{min} \cdots +_{min} S_J$$
4. Return the MIN-expression F'.

Theorem # 6.6 *If F_{n_i} denotes the MAX-expression of the ith child of the MIN-node n, then the MIN-expression of the node n is:*
$$F_n = \text{MAX-to-MIN}(F_{n_1}) +_{min} \text{MAX-to-MIN}(F_{n_2}) +_{min} \cdots +_{min} \text{MAX-to-MIN}(F_{n_m})$$
where m denotes the number of children of node n.
Proof: On lines similar to the proof of theorem 6.5. □

At the leaf nodes of the game tree, the values themselves are the packets. Using the MAX-to-MIN and MIN-to-MAX functions and the absorption laws, we can now compute (in a bottom-up manner) the minimal set of packets at each node of the game tree (and ultimately those at the root node). Let us consider an example.

Example # 6.5 Consider the game tree in Fig 6.6. Let F_i denote the MAX-expression at the MAX-node i and the MIN-expression at the MIN-node i. It is easy to see that $F_4 = \{(5, 4)\} +_{min} \{(3, 10)\}$ and $F_5 = \{(11, 5)\} +_{min} \{(5, 9)\}$. Therefore, MIN-to-MAX($F_4$) is $\{(5, 4), (3, 10)\}$ and MIN-to-MAX(F_5) is $\{(11, 5), (5, 9)\}$. The MAX-expression F_3 can be computed as:

$$F_3 = \{(5, 4), (3, 10)\} +_{max} \{(11, 5), (5, 9)\} = \{(11, 5), (5, 9)\}$$

Likewise, it is easy to see that $F_7 = \{(12, 7)\} +_{min} \{(7, 12)\}$ and $F_8 = \{(13, 6)\} +_{min} \{(6, 13)\}$. Therefore, MIN-to-MAX($F_7$) is $\{(12, 7), (7, 12)\}$ and MIN-to-MAX(F_8) is $\{(13, 6), (6, 13)\}$. The MAX-expression F_6 can be computed as:

$$F_6 = \{(12, 7), (7, 12)\} +_{max} \{(13, 6), (6, 13)\}$$

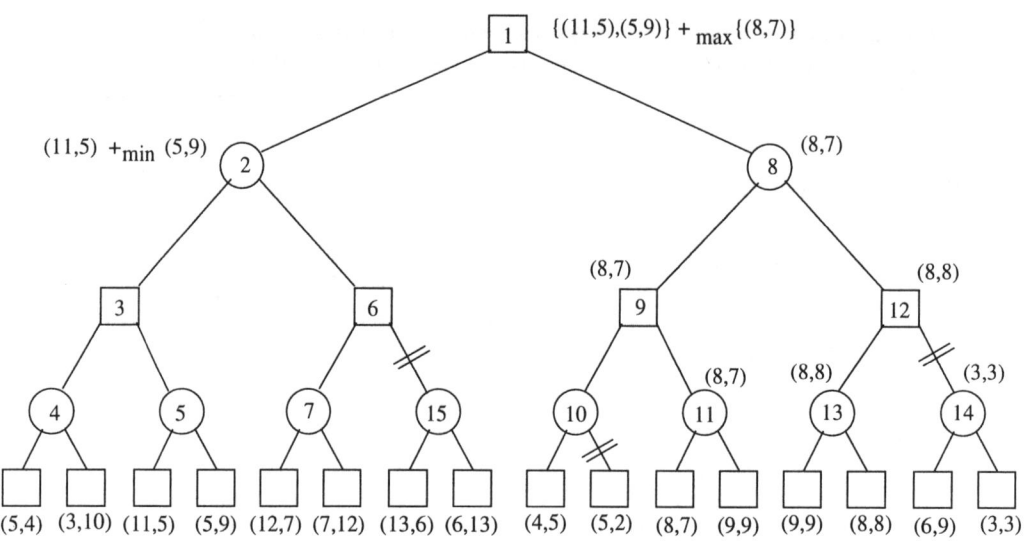

Figure 6.6: A Multiobjective Game Tree

MAX-to-MIN(F_3) can be computed as $\{(11,5)\} +_{min} \{(5,9)\}$. Also, MAX-to-MIN($F_6$) can be computed as:

$$\{(12,7),(13,6)\} +_{min} \{(12,7),(6,13)\} +_{min} \{(7,12),(13,6)\} +_{min} \{(7,12),(6,13)\}$$

The MIN-expression F_2 can now be computed as:

$$\begin{aligned} F_2 &= \{(12,7),(13,6)\} +_{min} \{(12,7),(6,13)\} +_{min} \{(7,12),(13,6)\} \\ &\quad +_{min} \{(7,12),(6,13)\} +_{min} \{(11,5)\} +_{min} \{(5,9)\} \\ &= \{(11,5)\} +_{min} \{(5,9)\} \end{aligned}$$

Looking at the other side of the game tree, the MIN-expression at node 10 is $F_{10} = \{(4,5)\} +_{min} \{(5,2)\}$ and that at node 11 (using MIN-absorption law) is $F_{11} = \{(8,7)\}$. Using, the MIN-to-MAX function on F_{10} and F_{11} we obtain the MAX-expression at node 9 as follows:

$$F_9 = \{(4,5),(5,2)\} +_{max} \{(8,7)\} = \{(8,7)\}$$

Similarly, using MIN-absorption law we have $F_{13} = \{(8,8)\}$ and $F_{14} = \{(3,3)\}$. Therefore the MAX-expression at node 12 is:

$$F_{12} = \{(8,8)\} +_{max} \{(3,3)\} = \{(8,8)\}$$

The MIN-expression at node 8 can now be computed as:

$$F_8 = \{(8,7)\} +_{min} \{(8,8)\} = \{(8,7)\}$$

Now, MIN-to-MAX(F_2) is $\{(11,5),(5,9)\}$ and MIN-to-MAX(F_8) is $\{(8,7)\}$. Therefore, the MAX-expression at node 1 is:

$$F_1 = \{(11,5),(5,9)\} +_{max} \{(8,7)\}$$

Thus at the root node of the game tree of Fig 6.6, player-1 has two packets to choose from, namely $\{(11,5),(5,9)\}$ and $\{(8,7)\}$. □

6.4 Partial Order α-β Pruning

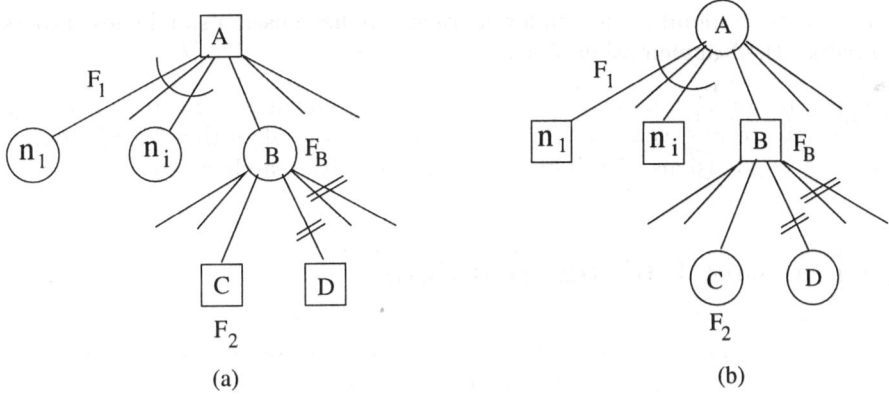

Figure 6.7: Shallow Pruning

6.4 Partial Order α-β Pruning

In the previous section, we have seen how the set of non-dominated packets can be identified. However, the bottom-up approach is a brute force method that may require too much time and space. If we can find out conditions under which certain branches of the game tree can be pruned, then we can apply techniques similar to α-β pruning to achieve our objective more efficiently.

We define two boolean functions *max_prune(F_1, F_2)* and *min_prune(F_1, F_2)* as follows:

Def # 6.4 [Dominance Test for Pruning]

max_prune(F_1, F_2): *If every packet in the MAX-expression F_2 is absorbed by the MAX-expression F_1 using clear dominance (of the MAX-absorption law), then max_prune(F_1, F_2) is true, else it is false.*

min_prune(F_1, F_2): *If every packet in the MIN-expression F_2 is absorbed by the MIN-expression F_1 using clear dominance (of the MIN-absorption law), then min_prune(F_1, F_2) is true, else it is false.*

Using the above functions, we define pruning conditions in partial order game trees which are somewhat analogous to α-β pruning in conventional game trees.

6.4.1 Shallow α-β pruning

The following lemmas help in identifying shallow pruning conditions.

Lemma # 6.4 *Consider the situation as in the game tree in Fig 6.7 (a). F_1 denotes the MAX-expression obtained at node A by collecting the packets (for player-1) backed up by the children $n_1, \ldots, n_i$ only. F_2 denotes the MAX-expression for the entire set of packets (for player-1) backed up at node C. F_B denotes the MIN-expression for the entire set of packets backed up (for player-2) at node B. If max_prune(F_1, F_2) is true, then the following equality holds.*

$$F_1 +_{max} MIN\_to\_MAX(F_B) = F_1$$

Proof: Let us assume the contrary. Then there exists a packet P in MIN-to-MAX(F_B) which cannot be absorbed by F_1. This means that if player-1 takes the move to B, there exists a strategy of player-1 to reach an outcome in P or some outcome which dominates an outcome in P. Thus, even if player-2 takes the move to C, then there exists a subset P' of P, such that player-1 is able to reach some outcome in P' (or some outcome that dominates an outcome in P'). Therefore P' is either a packet at node C, or dominated by some packet at node C. In either case, P' can be absorbed by some packet P_i in F_1 using clear dominance. Since P' is a subset of P, it follows that P can also be absorbed by P_i using clear dominance. This contradicts our assumption that the packet P cannot be absorbed by F_1. The result follows. □

Lemma 6.4 shows that shallow pruning can be effected on the other successors of node B when max_prune(F_1, F_2) is true, where F_1 and F_2 are as described in the statement of the lemma. It may be noted that in Fig 6.7 (a), if F_1 absorbs a packet of F_2 using freedom of choice (in the MAX-absorption law), then the pruning is not possible. For example, let F_1 be $\{(11,5)\} +_{max} \{(5,7)\}$ and F_2 be $\{(11,5),(5,7)\}$. Let the MAX-expression F_D at node D be $\{(2,9)\}$. Let there be no other children of node B (except nodes C and D). Then node B can back up the packet $\{(11,5),(5,7),(2,9)\}$ at node A, which cannot be absorbed by F_1. If node D would have been pruned, then this packet would not be backed up. This is the reason for our using only the clear dominance criteria (of the absorption laws) for defining the pruning conditions.

Using similar reasoning, we can define pruning conditions where the function min_prune is applicable.

Lemma # 6.5 *Consider the situation as in the game tree in Fig 6.7 (b). F_1 denotes the MIN-expression obtained at node A by collecting the packets (for player-2) backed up by the children $n_1, \ldots, n_i$ only. F_2 denotes the MIN-expression for the entire set of packets (for player-2) backed up at node C. F_B denotes the MAX-expression for the entire set of packets backed up (for player-1) at node B. If min_prune(F_1, F_2) is true, then the following equality holds.*

$$F_1 +_{min} MAX\_to\_MIN(F_B) = F_1$$

Proof: On lines similar to the proof of lemma 6.4. □

6.4 Partial Order α-β Pruning

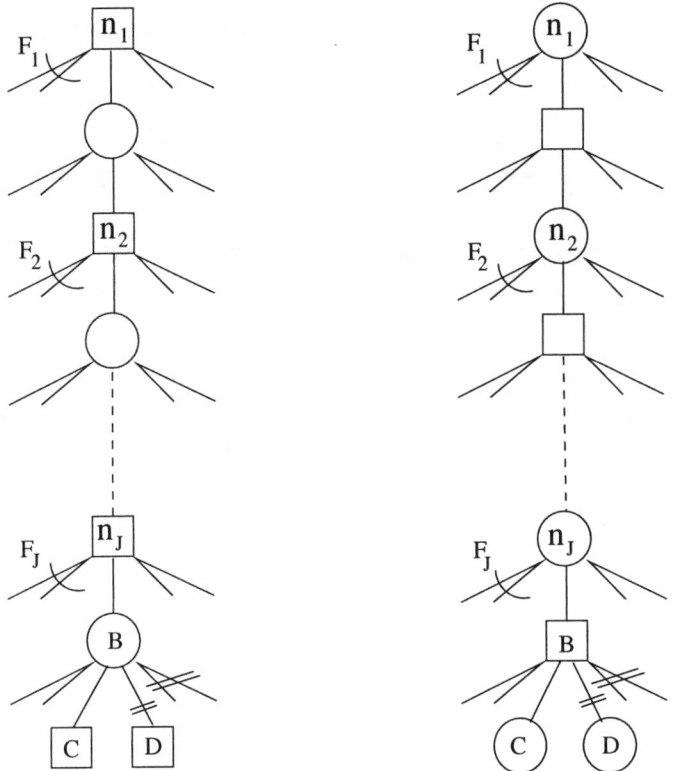

Figure 6.8: Deep Pruning

6.4.2 Deep α-β pruning

Deep pruning conditions can also be identified for partial order game trees as follows.

Lemma # 6.6 *Consider a path in a game tree as shown in Fig 6.8 (a). F_i denotes the MAX-expression formed by collecting the set of packets (for player-1) backed up by those children of MAX-node n_i which are to the left of the child in the given path. F_C denotes the set of packets (for player-1) at node C. Let F denote the following MAX-expression:*

$$F = F_1 +_{max} F_2 +_{max} \cdots +_{max} F_J$$

If $max\_prune(F, F_C)$ is true, then at node n_J, the move to node B will never be selected by player-1.

Proof: Let us assume the contrary, that is, player-1 selects the move to node B when the game reaches node n_J. Since player-2 can then select the move to node C, therefore, it is easy to see that each packet (for player-1) backed up by node B to n_J must contain a subset which is either a packet at node C or dominated by a packet at node C.

In the partial order game tree search problem, player-1 will have a set of packets of outcomes to choose from at the root node n_1. By definition, if the player-1 selects a packet, then there exists a strategy for it to ensure that the final outcome is either some outcome from that set or dominates some outcome from that set. Therefore, if the strategy of player-1 is such that it selects the packet P from the set of packets at the root node, then the game will go through those MAX-nodes n_i that has a non-dominated packet which is either some subset of P, or dominates some subset of P (and therefore, dominates P).

Therefore, if the game reaches node B, then player-1 must have selected a packet P at the root node such that there exists a packet P' (for player-1) backed up by node B to node n_J which is either a subset of P or dominates P. It follows that in each node n_i in the path to n_J, there exists a non-dominated packet P_i such that either P' is a subset of P_i, or P' dominates P_i.

Since P' is a packet backed up by node B, it contains a subset which is either a packet P_c at node C or dominated by a packet P_c at node C. Since min_prune(F, F_C) is true, therefore there exists a packet P'_i at some node n_i which dominates P_c using clear dominance. P'_i will then also dominate P' and therefore, will dominate P_i. Thus P_i is a dominated packet at node n_i which brings us to a contradiction. The result follows. □

Using similar reasoning, we can prove the following lemma.

Lemma # 6.7 *Consider a path in a game tree as shown in Fig 6.8 (b). F_i denotes the MIN-expression formed by collecting the set of packets (for player-2) backed up by those children of MIN-node n_i which are to the left of the child in the given path. F_C denotes the set of packets (for player-2) at node C. Let F denote the following MAX-expression:*

$$F = F_1 +_{min} F_2 +_{min} \cdots +_{min} F_J$$

If min_prune(F, F_C) is true, then at node n_J, the move to node B will never be selected by player-1.
Proof: On lines similar to the proof of lemma 6.6. □

Lemma 6.6 and lemma 6.7 allows us to define α-expressions for MIN-nodes and β-expressions for MAX-nodes (using the idea of the α and β bounds in conventional game tree search).

Def # 6.5 α-expression:
The α-expression at a MIN-node B is the MAX-expression formed by collecting the packets (for player-1) currently backed up at all MAX ancestors of B.

Lemma 6.6 shows that the exploration of a MIN-node B can be terminated as soon as the MAX-expression backed up by any of its children is absorbed by the α-expression at B (using clear dominance).

6.4 Partial Order α-β Pruning

Def # 6.6 β-expression:
The β-expression at a MAX-node B is the MIN-expression formed by collecting the packets (for player-2) currently backed up at all MIN ancestors of B.

Lemma 6.7 shows that the exploration of a MAX-node B can be terminated as soon as the MIN-expression backed up by any of its children is absorbed by the β-expression at B (using clear dominance).

Using these results, we may now develop an algorithm on lines similar to the α-β pruning algorithm of conventional game tree search. Given heuristic vector estimates $e(n)$ at each terminal node n, the following procedure uses a technique similar to α-β pruning to determine the set of non-dominated packets for player-1. The call $F(s, -\vec{\infty}, +\vec{\infty})$ returns the MAX-expression at node s. $+\vec{\infty}$ is a packet containing a single K-dimensional outcome which has all dimensions equal to $+\infty$. Likewise $-\vec{\infty}$ is a packet containing a single K-dimensional outcome which has all dimensions equal to $-\infty$.

procedure $F(n, \alpha, \beta)$
1. IF n is a terminal node THEN Return $e(n)$

2. Generate successors $m_1, m_2, \ldots, m_b$ of n
    2.1 Set $i \leftarrow 1$
    2.2 IF n is a MAX-node THEN
        2.2.1 Set $F_n \leftarrow -\vec{\infty}$
        2.2.2 Set $F_{m_i} \leftarrow F(m_i, \alpha, \beta)$
            If $F_{m_i} = -\vec{\infty}$ THEN Goto [Step 2.2.4], ELSE:
            2.2.2.1 Set $\alpha \leftarrow \alpha +_{max} F_{m_i}$
            2.2.2.2 Set $F_n \leftarrow F_n +_{max} F_{m_i}$
        2.2.3 IF min_prune(β,MAX-to-MIN(F_{m_i})) is true THEN Return $-\vec{\infty}$
        2.2.4 IF $i = b$ THEN Return F_n
            ELSE Set $i \leftarrow i + 1$ and Goto [Step 2.2.2]
    2.3 IF n is a MIN-node THEN
        2.3.1 Set $F_n \leftarrow +\vec{\infty}$
        2.3.2 Set $F_{m_i} \leftarrow F(m_i, \alpha, \beta)$
            If $F_{m_i} = -\vec{\infty}$ THEN Goto [Step 2.3.4], ELSE:
            2.3.2.1 Set $\beta \leftarrow \beta +_{min}$ MAX-to-MIN(F_{m_i})
            2.3.2.2 Set $F_n \leftarrow F_n +_{min}$ MAX-to-MIN(F_{m_i})
        2.3.3 IF max_prune(α, F_{m_i}) is true THEN Return $-\vec{\infty}$
        2.3.4 IF $i = b$ THEN Return MIN-to-MAX(F_n)
            ELSE Set $i \leftarrow i + 1$ and Goto [Step 2.3.2]

The working of the algorithm is illustrated on the game tree of Fig 6.6. The sequence of nodes visited, and the corresponding values of α and β is as shown in table 6.1. In MAX-nodes, $F(n)$ denotes the MAX-expression and in MIN-nodes, $F(n)$ denotes the MIN-expression. For convenience of writing, we have written packets containing a single outcome (a, b) as "(a, b)" instead of "$\{(a, b)\}$".

n	F(n)	α	β
n_1, n_2, n_3	–	$-\vec{\infty}$	$+\vec{\infty}$
n_4	(5,4) $+_{min}$ (3,10)	$-\vec{\infty}$	(5,4) $+_{min}$ (3,10)
n_3	–	{(5,4),(3,10)}	$+\vec{\infty}$
n_5	(11,5) $+_{min}$ (5,9)	{(5,4),(3,10)}	(11,5) $+_{min}$ (5,9)
n_3	{(5,4),(3,10)} $+_{max}$ {(11,5),(5,9)} = {(11,5),(5,9)}	{(11,5),(5,9)}	$+\vec{\infty}$
n_2, n_6	–	$-\vec{\infty}$	(11,5) $+_{min}$ (5,9)
n_7	(12,7) $+_{min}$ (7,12)	$-\vec{\infty}$	(11,5) $+_{min}$ (5,9) $+_{min}$ (12,7) $+_{min}$ (7,12) = (11,5) $+_{min}$ (5,9)
* n_6	–	{(12,7),(7,12)}	(11,5) $+_{min}$ (5,9)
n_2	(11,5) $+_{min}$ (5,9)	$-\vec{\infty}$	(11,5) $+_{min}$ (5,9)
n_1, n_8, n_9	–	{(11,5),(5,9)}	$+\vec{\infty}$
* n_{10}	–	{(11,5),(5,9)}	(4,5)
n_9	–	{(11,5),(5,9)}	$+\vec{\infty}$
n_{11}	(8,7) $+_{min}$ (9,9) = (8,7)	{(11,5),(5,9)}	(8,7)
n_9	(8,7)	{(11,5),(5,9)}	$+\vec{\infty}$
n_8, n_{12}	–	{(11,5),(5,9)}	(8,7)
n_{13}	(9,9) $+_{min}$ (8,8) = (8,8)	{(11,5),(5,9)}	(8,7) $+_{min}$ (8,8) = (8,7)
* n_{12}	–	{(11,5),(5,9)} $+_{max}$ (8,8)	(8,7)
n_8	(8,7)	{(11,5),(5,9)}	(8,7)
n_1	{(11,5),(5,9)} $+_{max}$ (8,7)	{(11,5),(5,9)} $+_{max}$ (8,7)	$+\vec{\infty}$

* Pruning occurs at these nodes.

Table 6.1: Sequence of nodes visited by *procedure F* on the game tree of Fig

6.5 Conclusion

The partial order game tree search problem studied in this chapter is inherent in many games of moderate complexity. However, before such a scheme can be put into practice, the pruning conditions and basic search strategies should be tuned to cater to the formulations of specific problems. For example, it is likely that if a problem involves many criteria, and each of them are modeled as separate dimensions of the cost vector, then very little pruning is possible as most outcomes become non-dominated. In order to enhance the pruning in such situations a judicious combination of some of the criteria may be called for. In the other extreme case, when all the criteria can be meaningfully combined, the pruning conditions presented in this chapter collapses to the pruning conditions of total order game tree search.

Chapter 7

Conclusion

In this book we have considered three different representation schemes within the multiobjective search framework, namely the state space, problem reduction and game tree representations. We have studied each representation individually and have analyzed the possibility of extending standard search techniques to this framework with suitable modifications. Interestingly our attempts in this direction have led to entirely different situations in the three representation schemes.

- In the multiobjective state space search representation, we have observed that standard search techniques developed for the conventional model may be extended to the multiobjective domain with suitable modifications. Consequently standard properties of the basic search model such as *pathmax* are also applicable to the multiobjective techniques. We have also observed that once the basic problem of multiple cost back-up is resolved, known memory bounded search techniques can be extended to the multiobjective state space search problem.

- The multiobjective AND/OR graph search problem presents an entirely different picture from that of state space search. For this representation we have shown that the multiobjective model itself differs from the conventional model in some of the basic aspects. In particular we have established that unlike in the conventional model, the task of best-first selection in the multiobjective AND/OR graph search problem is NP-hard in general. This property of the multiobjective problem effectively implies that simply extending standard techniques from the conventional framework may not yield multiobjective strategies having the same desirable properties.

- Whereas the problems of multiobjective state space search and multiobjective problem reduction search originate from multicriteria optimization problems, the multiobjective game tree search problem follows not only from multiobjective searching in the presence of an adversary, but also from conventional game playing situations where the individual judgement and experience of a player play a major role in the decision making. We have shown that in such game playing situations the information shared amongst the players is effectively a partial order on the states of the game. This leads to a partial order game tree search problem where the estimates computed at the leaf nodes of the game tree are vectors.

In this section we shall briefly discuss the results presented in this book on multiobjective heuristic search and the scope for future research in this area.

Stewart and White [90, 91] had shown that several desirable properties of A^* extend to their algorithm MOA^*. The results presented in chapter 3 further show that several other techniques (such as *pathmax*) can be adapted from the conventional search model to develop effective multiobjective search strategies. Our results also show that the multiobjective model presents properties of its own which need to be considered before known search schemes can be extended to this framework.

In this work we have presented some results on multiobjective state space search using non-monotone and inadmissible heuristics. The results presented on these lines (in chapter 3) are as follows.

- In the multiobjective search framework, the use of *pathmax* may reduce the number of nodes expanded by an algorithm such as MOA^* even in *non-pathological* tree search instances.

- When the heuristics are inadmissible, no algorithm is guaranteed to find all non-dominated solutions unless it expands nodes having dominated costs also.

The first result shows that *pathmax* has a greater significance in the multiobjective framework than in the conventional model. Though we find this result quite interesting, it may not have much practical significance since most well constructed heuristic functions are actually monotonic in nature. The other result reveals a situation which requires further investigation to determine the best strategies for multiobjective state space search with inadmissible heuristics. We have presented some preliminary analysis on the conditions of admissibility of strategies such as MOA^* using inadmissible heuristics.

Our investigations on the utility of an induced total order to guide the partial order search mechanism has led to several interesting results. Since conventional search strategies are based on a total order on the node costs, the use of an induced total order in the multiobjective framework is in a way a key to extend those strategies to the multiobjective framework. This was the general idea behind the policy of using the total order. The results presented in chapter 3 and chapter 5 establish that when an induced total order is used to guide the search the following benefits may be obtained.

- It is not necessary in general to compute every heuristic vector at a node. The result holds both for ordinary and AND/OR graphs.

- It is possible for a memory bounded strategy to guarantee admissibility inspite of backing up only one cost vector from an arbitrarily large set of non-dominated cost vectors in the pruned space. The result holds for searching ordinary graphs as well as AND/OR graphs.

- In multiobjective search of AND/OR graphs the policy of using an induced total order to select the successor of every OR-node ensures that the selected *psg* is non-dominated. Merely selecting non-dominated successors does not ensure non-dominance of the *psg*.

While the use of an induced total order appears to be beneficial in multiobjective state space search, as well as in multiobjective search of AND/OR graphs, the multiobjective game tree search problem presents a different picture. In that problem we have shown that when the preferences of one player (which is effectively a mapping of the states of the game to a total order) is known, these preferences cannot be safely used at the interior nodes of the game tree.

Throughout the chapters 3, 4 and 5 we have used *K-ordering* to represent the induced total order on the search. It appears that the results related to K-ordering will also hold for any general induced total order. However, there may be some other properties which may justify the use of some specific total order. For example some particular total order might be better suited to the type of data structures being used by the search mechanism.

The multiobjective state space search strategies MOA^{**} and $MOMA^*0$ that were presented in chapter 3 follow from known single objective search strategies such as A^* [69], MA^* [10] and $RBFS$ [51] with suitable modifications (such as the use of *K-ordering*). The experimental results presented in chapter 4 provide empirical evidence of the fact that the strategies MOA^{**} and $MOMA^*0$ are much better suited to the multiobjective problem than straight-forward extensions of single objective strategies such as A^* and $DFBB$.

Though the multiobjective state space search problem presents several interesting properties of its own, it has been possible to generalize algorithms such as A^* to the multiobjective framework because none of the properties of the multiobjective problem causes any major difficulties in the way of extending the desirable properties of established single objective strategies to this framework. On the other hand, in the multiobjective AND/OR graph search problem, we have shown (in chapter 5) that the search model itself has the following property which rules out the possibility of extending some of the desirable properties of best-first strategies such as AO^* to the multiobjective problem.

- Given an explicit AND/OR graph, the task of identifying a non-dominated cost *psg* is NP-hard in general.

By virtue of this result we have shown in chapter 5 that unless $P = NP$, it will not be possible in general to develop a search strategy for the multiobjective problem whose complexity is polynomial in the number of nodes belonging to non-dominated *psgs*, unlike in the single objective problem where the worst case complexity of AO^* is polynomial in the number of nodes belonging to psgs whose cost is less than or equal to the cost of the optimal solution graph.

The steps leading to the algorithm $MObj^*$ for searching multiobjective AND/OR graphs were decided on the basis of two policies. The first was to revise the costs of only those psgs that are born out of the current psg by expanding one of its tip nodes. The other was to perform the search in linear space by retaining only the current psg in the memory. Both these policies are ad-hoc schemes that appear to be useful from the arguments presented in chapter 5. The task of developing better strategies for the problem remains open.

The multiobjective game tree search problem considered in chapter 6 is an interesting variant of the conventional game tree search problem. This problem originates from the fact that in many practical game playing situations the information shared amongst the players is a partial order. Similar situations also arise in multicriteria game playing situations. The analysis presented in chapter 6 reveals that under the realistic assumption that each player knows its own game playing strategy but not that of its opponent, the individual preferences of a player cannot be used in the interior nodes of the game tree. We have shown that partial order search may be used to determine the set of non-inferior options corresponding to each move of the player at the root node of the game tree. Thereafter the strategy of the player may be used to determine the best move.

Dominance algebra (presented in chapter 6) is only a convenient way of representing the relation between the various packets at a node. The $+_{max}$ and $+_{min}$ operators combined with the MAX and MIN absorption laws provide a comprehensible scheme to represent the equivalent of MIN-MAX (of conventional game tree search). The same results could also be presented in algorithmic terms. However, we feel that *dominance algebra* conveys the basic issues in more clear terms.

The pruning conditions described in chapter 6 for the partial order game tree search problem are general pruning conditions that apply to conventional game trees as well. The generalization of the α-β pruning strategy presented in the same chapter uses these pruning conditions to determine the set of non-dominated packets for the player at the root node. An important aspect which has not been taken up in this work is the use of this strategy or its variants in actual game playing situations. This remains an important and interesting future work.

Though the general multiobjective search schemes presented in this book are applicable to problems with any number of objectives, some very important issues need to be investigated before applying these schemes to a given problem. Two of the most important issues are as follows:

- If the given problem has many objectives and each of these criteria are mapped into distinct dimensions of the cost vector then it is likely that most of the solution nodes have non-dominated cost vectors. This may necessitate the problem solver to judiciously combine some of the less important objectives (based on user preferences which may be obtained during search) and allow the more important criteria to be mapped into distinct dimensions of the cost vector. Once this is done, the search schemes presented in this book may be used effectively.

- Development of effective data structures for multiobjective search schemes is one problem which needs to be well studied before the model can be put into general practice.

In this book we have considered only three practical multi-criteria optimization problems. Since such problems are numerous the scope of applicability of multiobjective heuristic search techniques is vast. Parallelization of multiobjective search techniques appears promising due to the presence of multiple non-dominated search avenues that may be explored simultaneously without fear of over-expansion.

Appendix A

A.1 The outline of algorithm MOMA*

The following is the outline of the algorithm MOMA*. The algorithm uses a parameter called MAX which indicates the number of nodes that are allowed to be retained in the memory. The algorithm uses a variable called *node_count* to count the number of nodes currently retained in the memory.

Algorithm MOMA*

1. [INITIALIZE]
    OPEN $\leftarrow$ s ; CLOSED $\leftarrow \phi$;
    SOLUTION_GOALS $\leftarrow \phi$; SOLUTION_COSTS $\leftarrow \phi$;
    node_count $\leftarrow$ 0
    Compute the set of cost vectors of s.
    Assign the representative vector of s to $F(s)$ and each $F_i(s)$.

2. [TERMINATE]
    If OPEN is empty then Terminate.

3. [SELECT 1]
    3.1 Remove the node n in OPEN with minimum F(n) in K-order.
    3.2 Resolve ties in favor of the goal nodes, else in favor of nodes at a greater depth.
    3.3 Set $GL \leftarrow F(n)$

4. [DOMINANCE CHECK]
    If $F(n)$ is dominated by the cost vector of a solution in SOLUTION_COSTS then
        4.1 Compute the next representative cost vector of n.
            4.1.1 If there is no such non-dominated vector then
                4.1.1.1 Discard node n.
                4.1.1.2 Goto [Step 2].
            4.1.2 Otherwise return n to OPEN and Goto [Step 3].

5. **[IDENTIFY SOUTIONS]**
    If n is a goal node then
    5.1 Put its cost vector in SOLUTION_COSTS.
    5.2 Output the solution.
    5.3 Set $F(n) \leftarrow \infty$
    5.4 Goto [Step 2]

6. **[EXPAND]**
    6.1 Expand n generating all its successors.
    6.2 For each successor n_j of n, do the following:
        6.2.1 Compute the representative cost vector $F(n_j)$ of n.
        6.2.2 Assign the vector $F(n_j)$ to each $F_i(n_j)$
        6.2.3 Set $F_j(n) \leftarrow F(n_j)$
        6.2.4 Enter n_j in OPEN
        6.2.5 Increment node_count
    6.3 Put n in CLOSED

7. **[SELECT 2]**
    7.1 Select the successor m of n with minimum $F(m)$ in K-order.
    7.2 If $F(m) \leq GL$ then select m for expansion and call it n.
    7.3 Goto [Step 4].

8. **[COST_REVISION]**
    8.1 Put the node m in a set Z
    8.2 Repeat the following steps until Z is empty.
        8.2.1 Remove the node p from Z. Let q be its parent and p be the jth successor of q.
        8.2.2 Set $F_j(q) \leftarrow F(p)$
        8.2.3 Let $F_{min}(q)$ denote the minimum among all $F_i(q)$ in K-order.
        8.2.4 If $F(q) < F_{min}(q)$ then
            8.2.4.1 Set $F(q) \leftarrow F_{min}(q)$
            8.2.4.2 Put q in Z

9. **[CONTINUE]**
    9.1 If node_count $\leq$ MAX then Goto [Step 2]

10. **[PRUNING]**
    10.1 Select the leaf node r in OPEN with largest $F(r)$ in K-order.
    10.2 If $F_1(r) = GL$ then Goto [Step 3].
    10.3 Remove r from OPEN and decrement node_count.
    10.4 Let t be the parent of r. If t is in CLOSED then
        10.4.1 Remove t from CLOSED and put it in OPEN
    10.5 Goto [Step 10.1]

Bibliography

[1] BAGCHI, A., AND A.MAHANTI. Search algorithms under different kinds of heuristics: A comparative study. *JACM 30*, 1 (1983), 1–21.

[2] BELL, D. E. Multiattribute utility functions: Decomposition using interpolation. *Management Science 25* (1979), 744–753.

[3] BELL, E. D., K.L.RALPH, AND EDS., H. *Conflicting Objectives in Decisions*. John Wiley, 1977.

[4] BERLINER, H., AND C.EBELING. Pattern knowledge and search: The suprem architecture. *Artificial Intelligence 38* (1989), 161–198.

[5] BOGETOFT, P. General communication schemes for multiattribute decsion making. *Euro. Jour. of Opl. Res. 26* (1986), 108–122.

[6] BRADY, M. L., AND D.J.BROWN. VLSI routing: Four layers suffice. *Advances Comput. Res. 2* (1984).

[7] BROCKHOFF, K. Experimental test of mcdm algorithms in a modular approach. *Euro. Jour. of Opl. Res. 22* (1985), 159–166.

[8] BROWN, T. A., AND R.E.STRAUCH. Dynamic programming in multiplicative lattices. *Jour. of Math. Anal. and Appl. 12* (1965), 364–370.

[9] BURSTEIN, M., AND R.PELAVIN. Hiearchical channel router. In *Proc. of 20th Design Automation Conference* (1983), pp. 591–597.

[10] CHAKRABARTI, P. P., S.GHOSE, A.ACHARYA, AND S.C.DESARKAR. Heuristic search in restricted memory. *Artificial Intelligence 41* (1989), 197–221.

[11] CHANG, C. L., AND J.R.SLAGLE. An admissible and optimal algorithm for searching AND/OR graphs. *Artificial Intelligence 2* (1971), 117–128.

[12] CHANGKONG, V., AND Y.Y.HAIMES. *Multiobjective Decision Making – Theory and Methodology*. North Holland, 1983.

[13] CHARNETSKI, J. R., AND R.M.SOLAND. Multiple attribute decision making with partial information. *Naval Res. Logistics Quart. 26* (1979), 249–256.

[14] COFFMAN, E. G. *Computer and Job Shop Scheduling Theory*. John Wiley, New York, 1976.

[15] COHON, J. L. *Multiobjective Programmming and Planning*. Academic Press, 1978.

[16] CONG, J., AND C.L.LIU. Over-the-cell channel routing. *IEEE Trans. on CAD 9* (1990), 408–418.

[17] CORLEY, H. W. Some simple multiobjective dynamic programs. *IEEE Trans. on Automatic Control 30* (1985), 1221–1222.

[18] DASGUPTA, P., P.MITRA, P.P.CHAKRABARTI, AND S.C.DESARKAR. Multiobjective search in $VLSI$ design. In *VLSI'94, Proc. of 7th Int. Conf. on VLSI Design, Calcutta, India* (1994), pp. 395–400.

[19] DASGUPTA, P., AND P.P.CHAKRABARTI. Heuristic search using multiple objectives. In *Proc. of 3rd National Seminar on Theoretical Computer Science, Kharagpur, India* (1993), pp. 352–364.

[20] DASGUPTA, P., P.P.CHAKRABARTI, AND S.C.DESARKAR. Game tree search under a partial order. In *Proc. of 4th National Seminar on Theoretical Computer Science, Kanpur, India* (1994), pp. 40–52.

[21] DASGUPTA, P., P.P.CHAKRABARTI, AND S.C.DESARKAR. Utility of *pathmax* in partial order heuristic search. *Information Processing Letters 55* (1995), 317–322.

[22] DASGUPTA, P., P.P.CHAKRABARTI, AND S.C.DESARKAR. Multiobjective heuristic search in AND/OR graphs. *Journal of Algorithms 20* (1996), 282–311.

[23] DASGUPTA, P., P.P.CHAKRABARTI, AND S.C.DESARKAR. New results on multiobjective state space search. *Sadhana 21*, 3 (1996), 263–290.

[24] DASGUPTA, P., P.P.CHAKRABARTI, AND S.C.DESARKAR. Searching game trees under a partial order. *Artificial Intelligence 82* (1996), 237–257.

[25] DECHTER, R., AND J.PEARL. Generalized best-first search strategies and the optimality of A^*. *JACM 32*, 3 (1985), 505–536.

[26] DEUTSCH, D. N. A dogleg channel router. In *Proc. of 13th Design Automation Conference* (1976), pp. 425–433.

[27] DYER, J. S., AND R.K.SARIN. Measurable multiattribute value functions. *Operations Research 27* (1979), 810–822.

[28] ESCHENAUER, H. A., J.KOSKI, AND A.OSYCZKA. Multicriteria optimization– fundamentals and motivation. In *Multicriteria Design Optimization*, H.Eschenauer, J.Koski, and A.Osyczka, Eds. Springer-Verlag, 1990.

[29] FERREIRA, J. S., M.A.NEVES, AND P.F.CASTRO. A two-phase roll cutting problem. *Euro. Jour. of Opl. Res. 44* (1990), 185–196.

[30] FRENCH, S. Interactive multiobjective programming: Its aims applications and demands. *Jour. of the Opl. Res. Soc. 35* (1984), 827–834.

[31] GELPERIN, D. On the optimality of A^*. *Artificial Intelligence 8* (1977), 69–76.

[32] GEOFFRION, A. M., J.S.DYER, AND A.FEINBERG. An interactive approach for multicriterion optimization. *Management Science 19* (1972), 357–368.

[33] GOICOCHEA, A., D.R.HANSEN, AND L.DUCKSTEIN. *Multiobjective Decision Analysis with Engineering and Business Applications*. John Wiley, 1982.

[34] HAIMES, Y. Y., AND V.CHANGKONG. *Decision Making with Multiple Objectives*. Springer-Verlag, 1985.

[35] HANNAN, E. L. Obtaining non-dominated priority vectors for multiple objective decision making problems with different combinations of cardinal and ordinal information. *IEEE Trans. on Sys. Man. and Cybernatics 11* (1981), 538–543.

[36] HENIG, M. I. Vector valued dynamic programming. *SIAM Journal of Control and Opt. 21* (1983), 490–499.

[37] HENIG, M. I. Optimal paths in graphs with stochastic or multidimensional weights. *Comm. of the ACM 28* (1985), 1242–1244.

[38] HO, T. T., S.S.IYENGAR, AND S.Q.ZHENG. A general greedy channel routing algorithm. *IEEE Trans. on CAD 10*, 2 (1991), 204–211.

[39] HOLMES, N., N.SHERWANI, AND M.SARRAFZADEH. Algorithms for three-layer over-the-cell channel routing. In *Proc. of ICCAD-91* (1991), pp. 428–431.

[40] HOLMES, N., N.SHERWANI, AND M.SARRAFZADEH. New algorithms for over-the-cell channel routing using vacant terminals. In *Proc. of 28th Design Automation Conference* (1991), pp. 126–131.

[41] HOROWITZ, E., AND S.SAHNI. *Fundamental Of Computer Algorithms*. Computer Science Press, 1984.

[42] HWANG, C. L., AND A.S.M.MASUD. *Multiobjective Decision Making – Methods and Applications*. Springer-Verlag, 1979.

[43] JAIN, R., A.C.PARKER, AND N.PARK. Predicting system level area and delay for pipelined and nonpipelined designs. *IEEE Trans. on CAD 11*, 8 (1992).

[44] JAIN, R., K.KUCUKCAKAR, M.J.MLINAR, AND A.C.PARKER. Experience with the ADAM synthesis system. In *Proc. of 26th Design Automation Conference* (1989).

[45] KEENEY, R. L., AND H.RAIFFA. *Decisions with Multiple Objectives: Preferences and Value Tradeoffs*. John Wiley, 1976.

[46] KNUTH, D. E., AND R.W.MOORE. An analysis of alpha-beta pruning. *Artificial Intelligence 6* (1975), 293–326.

[47] KOK, M. The interface with decsion makers and some experimental results in interactive multiple objective programming methods. *Euro. Jour. of Opl. Res. 26* (1986), 96–107.

[48] KORF, R. E. Depth-first iterative deepening: An optimal admissible tree search. *Artificial Intelligence 27* (1985), 97–109.

[49] KORF, R. E. Multiplayer alpha-beta pruning. *Artificial Intelligence 48* (1991), 99–111.

[50] KORF, R. E. Linear-space best-first search: Summary of results. In *Proc. of AAAI-92* (1992), pp. 533–538.

[51] KORF, R. E. Linear-space best-first search. *Artificial Intelligence 62* (1993), 41–78.

[52] KORHONEN, P. J. A heirarchical interactive method for ranking alternatives with multiple qualitative criteria. *Euro. Jour. of Opl. Res. 24* (1986), 265–276.

[53] KORHONEN, P. J. On using computer graphics for solving MCDM problems. In *Towards Interactive and Intelligent Decision Support Systems*, K. Y.Sawaragi and H.Nakayama, Eds. Springer-Verlag, 1987, pp. 154–162.

[54] KORHONEN, P. J., H.MOSKOWITZ, AND J.WALLENIUS. A progressive algorithm for modeling and solving multiple-criteria decision problems. *Operations Research 34* (1986), 726–731.

[55] KORHONEN, P. J., AND J.LAAKSO. A visual interactive method for solving the multiple criteria problem. *Euro. Jour. of Opl. Res. 24* (1986), 277–287.

[56] KRZYSZTOFOWICZ, R., AND L.DUCKSTEIN. Assessment errors in multiattribute utility functions. *Organizational Behavior and Human Performance 26* (1980), 326–348.

[57] KUMAR, A., KUMAR, A., AND M.BALAKRISHNAN. A novel integrated scheduling and allocation algorithm for data path synthesis. In *VLSI'94, Proc. of 4th Int. Conf. on VLSI Design* (1991), pp. 212–218.

[58] LEVINE, P., AND J.POMEROL. PRIAM: An iteractive program for choosing among multiple attribute alternatives. *Euro. Jour. of Opl. Res. 25* (1986), 272–280.

[59] LIPSKI, W. An NP-complete problem related to three-layer channel routing. *Advances Comput. Res. 2* (1984).

[60] MAREK-SADOWSKA, M. An unconstrained topological via minimization. *IEEE Trans. on CAD 3* (1984), 184–190.

[61] MARTELLI, A. On the complexity of admissible search algorithms. *Artificial Intelligence 8* (1977), 1–13.

[62] MARTELLI, A., AND U.MONTANARI. Additive AND/OR graphs. In *Proc. of 3rd Int. Joint Conf. on Artificial Intelligence, California* (1973), pp. 1–11.

[63] MARTELLI, A., AND U.MONTANARI. Optimising decision trees through heuristically guided search. *CACM 21*, 12 (1978), 1025–1039.

[64] MCFARLAND, M. C. Using bottom-up design techniques in the synthesis of digital hardware from abstract behavioral descriptions. In *Proc. of 23th Design Automation Conference* (1986).

[65] MCFARLAND, M. C., A.C.PARKER, AND R.CAMPOSANO. Tutorial on high-level synthesis. In *Proc. of 25th Design Automation Conference* (1988), pp. 330–336.

[66] MERO, L. A heuristic search algorithm with modifiable estimate. *Artificial Intelligence 23* (1984), 13–27.

[67] MOND, B., AND E.E.ROSINGER. Interactive weight assessment in multiple attribute decision making. *Euro. Jour. of Opl. Res. 22* (1985), 19–25.

[68] NILSSON, N. J. *Problem Solving Methods in Artificial Intelligence*. McGraw Hill, 1971.

[69] NILSSON, N. J. *Principles of Artificial Intelligence*. Tioga, Palo Alto, CA, 1980.

[70] OPPENHEIMER, K. R. A proxy approach to multiattribute decision making. *Management Science 24* (1978), 675–689.

[71] PAPADIMITRIOU, C. H., AND M.YANNAKAKIS. Shortest paths without a map. *Theoretical Computer Science 84* (1991), 127–150.

[72] PARKER, A. C., J.PIZARRO, AND M.J.MLINAR. MAHA: A program for datapath synthesis. In *Proc. of 23th Design Automation Conference* (1986).

[73] PAULIN, P. G., AND J.P.KNIGHT. Force directed scheduling for the behavioral synthesis of ASIC's. *IEEE Trans. on CAD June* (1989).

[74] PAULIN, P. G., J.P.KNIGHT, AND E.F.GIRCZYC. HAL: A multi-paradigm approach to automatic data path synthesis. In *Proc. of 23th Design Automation Conference* (1986).

[75] PEARL, J. *Heuristics: Intelligent Search Strategies for Computer Problem Solving*. Addison Wesley, 1984.

[76] PHILLIP, J. Algorithms for the vector maximization problem. *Math. Prog. 2* (1972), 207–229.

[77] PREPARATA, F. P., AND W.LIPSKI. Optimal three layer channel routing. *IEEE Trans. on Computers C-33* (1984), 5.

[78] RAMESH, R., S.ZIONTS, AND M.H.KARWAN. A class of practical interactive branch-and-bound algorithms for multicriteria integer programming. *Euro. Jour. of Opl. Res. 26* (1986), 161–172.

[79] RAO, V. N., V.KUMAR, AND R.E.KORF. Depth-first vs best-first search. In *Proc of AAAI-91* (1991), pp. 434–440.

[80] RIVEST, R. L., AND C.M.FIDUCCIA. A greedy channel router. In *Proc. of 19th Design Automation Conference* (1982), pp. 418–424.

[81] RUSSEL, S. Efficient memory-bounded search methods. In *Proc of ECAI-92* (1992).

[82] SARKAR, U. K., P.P.CHAKRABARTI, S.GHOSE, AND S.C.DESARKAR. Multiple stack branch and bound. *Information Processing Letters 37*, 1 (1991), 43–48.

[83] SARKAR, U. K., P.P.CHAKRABARTI, S.GHOSE, AND S.C.DESARKAR. Reducing reexpansions in iterative deepening search by controlling cutoff bounds. *Artificial Intelligence 50* (1991), 207–221.

[84] SARKAR, U. K., P.P.CHAKRABARTI, S.GHOSE, AND S.C.DESARKAR. Effective use of memory in iterative deepening search. *Information Processing Letters 42* (1992), 47–52.

[85] SARRAFZADEH, M., AND D.T.LEE. A new approach to topological via minimization. *IEEE Trans. on CAD 8* (1989), 890–900.

[86] SCHOEMAKER, P. J. H., AND C.C.WAID. An experimental comparison of different approaches to determining weights in additive utility models. *Management Science 28* (1982), 182–196.

[87] SEN, A. K., AND A.BAGCHI. Fast recursive formulations for best-first-search that allow controlled use of memory. In *Proc. IJCAI-89* (1989), pp. 297–302.

[88] SPRONK, J., AND S.ZIONTS. Special issue on multiple criteria decision making. *Management Science 30* (1984).

[89] STEUER, R. E. *Multiple Criteria Optimization: Theory, Computation and Application.* John Wiley, 1986.

[90] STEWART, B. S. *Heuristic Search with a General Order Relation.* PhD thesis, Univ. of Virginia, Charlottesville, 1988.

[91] STEWART, B. S., AND C.C.WHITE. Multiobjective A^*. *JACM 38*, 4 (1991), 775–814.

[92] STOCKMAN, G. A minmax algorithm better than alpha-beta ? *Artificial Intelligence 12* (1979), 179–196.

[93] TAKESHI, Y., AND E.S.KUH. Efficient algorithms for channel routing. *IEEE Trans. on CAD 1*, 1 (1982), 298–307.

[94] VANSNICK, J. C. On the problem of weights in multiple criteria decision making. *Euro. Jour. of Opl. Res. 24* (1986), 288–294.

[95] WALLENIUS, J. Comparative evaluation of some interactive approaches to multicriteria optimization. *Management Science 21* (1975), 1387–1395.

[96] WEBER, M. A method of multiattribute decision making with incomplete information. *Management Science 31* (1985), 1365–1371.

[97] WHITE, C. C., AND A.P.SAGE. A multiple objective optimization-based approach to choicemaking. *IEEE Trans. on Sys., Man and Cybernetics* (1980), 315–326.

[98] WHITE, C. C., S.DOZONO, AND W.T.SCHERER. An interactive procedure for aiding multiattribute alternative selection. *Omega* (1983), 212–214.

[99] ZELENY, M. *Multiple Criteria Decision Making.* McGraw-Hill, 1982.

[100] ZELENY, M. Systems approach to multiple criteria decision making: Metaoptimum. In *Towards Interactive and Intelligent Decision Support Systems*, K. Y.Sawaragi and H.Nakayama, Eds. Springer-Verlag, 1987, pp. 28–37.

Index

admissibility
    of MOA**, 28
    of MObj*, 93
    of MOMA*0, 39
    pathmax preserves, 23, 82
    with inadmissible heuristics, 46
alpha expression, 116
alpha-beta pruning, 6, 113, 117
    deep, 115
    shallow, 113
AND node, 76, 88
AND/OR graph, 75–77
    additive, 78
    explicit, 77
    implicit, 77
ASAP schedule, 51

backtracking, 32, 34, 89
beta expression, 117
brute-force search, 19, 29

Canadian TSP, 98
channel routing, 49, 57
    Deutsch difficult, 69
    Manhattan mode, 57
cost
    partial order, 1
    total order, 1
cost back-up, 32, 34, 89
cost revision, 34
cost vector, 2, 3, 11, 98
    of solution graph, 77
    representative, 26, 89
cost vectors
    of a psg, 78
cutting pattern, 66

design space, 50
DFBB, 68
DFG, 51
dogleg, 57
dominance, 2, 12
    clear, 105
    freedom of choice, 105
    in games, 98
    loose, 12
    strict, 12
dominance algebra, 6, 107
dominance test, 34, 89, 113

eligible node, 45
eligible path, 45
expand, 15, 28, 47, 90

game tree, 97
GL, 33, 89

hardness results, 81, 85
heuristics
    admissible, 21, 78
    for channel routing, 62
    for operator scheduling, 56
    inadmissible, 43
    monotone, 21, 78
high level synthesis, 49, 50

ItrA*, 68

K-ordering, 24, 26
    advantages, 30, 32
    in AND/OR graphs, 79

layout synthesis, 49, 57
log cutting, 66

Minf, 34, 36, 89, 91
MOA*, 13, 14
MOA**, 27
MObj*, 86, 87, 90
MOMA*, 125
MOMA*0, 33, 35

netlist, 57
NEXT_MIN, 33, 89
node
    cost of, 13, 26
    cost vectors of, 20, 79
    goal, 13
    non-dominated, 25
    structure of, 33, 88
    surely expanded, 30
    terminal, 76

operator scheduling, 49–51
optimality of MOA**, 28
OR graph, 96
OR node, 76, 88
outcome, 98
    comparison of, 101
    packet of, 104
    vector valued, 99

packet, 104
    absorption of, 107, 109
    dominance, 106
    dominance of, 105
pathmax, 21, 22
    in AND/OR graph, 81
    multidimensional, 23
    selection using, 81
    utility of, 24, 81
pmax, 45
pmax-ordering, 45
problem reduction, 75
psg, 75, 77

SECOND_MIN, 89
solution graph, 77
    cost of, 77
strategy, 101

termination
    condition, 35, 90
    of MOA**, 29
    of MObj*, 94

via, 57, 59